SNAKE ROAD

Shawnee Books

Quick Reference Guide

Northern Cottonmouth (p. 30)

Plain-bellied Watersnake (p. 36)

Western Ribbonsnake (p. 40)

Ring-necked Snake (p. 44)

Rough Greensnake (p. 48)

Gray Ratsnake (p. 51)

Dekay's Brownsnake (p. 55)

North American Racer (p. 58)

Mississippi Green Watersnake (p. 62)

Eastern Copperhead (p. 65)

Timber Rattlesnake (p. 69)

Red-bellied Snake (p. 74)

Smooth Earthsnake (p. 78)

Common Gartersnake (p. 81)

Eastern Black Kingsnake (p. 84)

Common Wormsnake (p. 87)

Eastern Milksnake (p. 90)

Diamond-backed Watersnake (p. 93)

Red-bellied Mudsnake (p. 96)

Eastern Hog-nosed Snake (p. 98)

Flat-headed Snake (p. 102)

Common Watersnake (p. 105)

Scarletsnake (p. 108). *Photograph courtesy of Jake Scott.*

SNAKE ROAD

A FIELD GUIDE
TO THE SNAKES OF
LARUE–PINE HILLS

Joshua J. Vossler

SOUTHERN ILLINOIS UNIVERSITY PRESS | CARBONDALE

Southern Illinois University Press
www.siupress.com

Copyright © 2021 by Joshua J. Vossler

All rights reserved
Printed in the United States of America

24 23 22 21   5 4 3 2

Cover illustration and *frontispiece*: Plain-bellied Watersnake about to cross Snake Road in early spring.

Section dividers: Gray Ratsnake in a defensive posture (pp. xiv, 1); juvenile Timber Rattlesnake, coiled and rattling (pp. 28, 29); Timber Rattlesnake coiled in ambush pose (pp. 110, 111); Timber Rattlesnake, covered in duckweed from a recent swim (pp. 142, 143).

Library of Congress Cataloging-in-Publication Data
Names: Vossler, Joshua J., author.
Title: Snake Road : a field guide to the snakes of LaRue–Pine Hills / Joshua J. Vossler.
Description: Carbondale : Southern Illinois University Press, 2021. | Series: Shawnee books | Includes bibliographical references.
Identifiers: LCCN 2020036354 (print) | LCCN 2020036355 (ebook) | ISBN 9780809338054 (paperback) | ISBN 9780809338061 (ebook)
Subjects: LCSH: Snakes—Illinois—Shawnee National Forest.
Classification: LCC QL666.O6 V83 2021 (print) | LCC QL666.O6 (ebook) | DDC 597.9609773/992—dc23
LC record available at https://lccn.loc.gov/2020036354
LC ebook record available at https://lccn.loc.gov/2020036355

Contents

Preface ix
Acknowledgments xiii

Introduction
  What Is Snake Road? 3
  On Using This Book 5
  Setting Your Expectations 6
  Preparing to Visit Snake Road 14
  Travel Information 18
  Rules of the Road 21
  How You Can Help Conserve Snake Road 22
  A Note on Names 23
  A Note on the Photography 23
  On Visually Identifying Snakes 24

Part 1. Snakes of Snake Road
  1. Northern Cottonmouth (Venomous) 30
  2. Plain-bellied Watersnake 36
  3. Western Ribbonsnake 40
  4. Ring-necked Snake 44
  5. Rough Greensnake 48
  6. Gray Ratsnake 51
  7. Dekay's Brownsnake 55
  8. North American Racer 58
  9. Mississippi Green Watersnake 62
  10. Eastern Copperhead (Venomous) 65
  11. Timber Rattlesnake (Venomous) 69
  12. Red-bellied Snake 74
  13. Smooth Earthsnake 78
  14. Common Gartersnake 81
  15. Eastern Black Kingsnake 84
  16. Common Wormsnake 87
  17. Eastern Milksnake 90

18. Diamond-backed Watersnake 93
19. Red-bellied Mudsnake 96
20. Eastern Hog-nosed Snake 98
21. Flat-headed Snake 102
22. Common Watersnake 105
23. Scarletsnake 108

Part 2. How to Tell Similar Snakes Apart
Black Snakes 112
Northern Cottonmouth (Venomous) and Plain-bellied
    Watersnake 114
Northern Cottonmouth (Venomous) and Eastern
    Copperhead (Venomous) 117
North American Racer and Gray Ratsnake 121
Red-bellied Snake and Dekay's Brownsnake 124
Western Ribbonsnake and Common Gartersnake 126
Smooth Earthsnake and Flat-headed Snake 128
Common Wormsnake and Smooth Earthsnake 130
Mississippi Green Watersnake and Diamond-backed
    Watersnake 132
Eastern Copperhead (Venomous) and Common
    Watersnake 134
Eastern Milksnake and Scarletsnake 138

Some Final Thoughts 145
Species Checklist 147
Further Reading 151

Preface

To me, there has never been a clear line between spending time outside and looking for snakes. Some people go bird watching. Others seek out wildflowers or scenic views. But my favorite activity is snake watching. As a boy I always felt an affinity for snakes. Where I grew up good snake habitat was hard to find, however, and my opportunity to observe these interesting reptiles in the wild was limited to the occasional Common Gartersnake or Smooth Greensnake glimpsed in a state park or wooded fishing pond. So while my interest in snakes never went away, there wasn't much opportunity for it to flourish. I was a wannabe snake watcher, limited to browsing field guides and hoping for a rare sighting to leap, or to slither, off the page.

Then, in 2014, I received an offer for a position in Morris Library at Southern Illinois University Carbondale. The job sounded exciting, but I had a hard time working up any enthusiasm for the location. I wrongly imagined southern Illinois as a windswept cornfield, devoid of wildlife habitat. My mother soon grew tired of my grousing and started researching the area. We discovered to our surprise that southern Illinois offered a wide variety of outdoor nature activities. My hopes rose. Some of the cypress swamps farthest to the north were being restored, and the high annual rainfall and mild winter temperatures made for a diverse flora and fauna. The rocky bluffs were like miniature mountain ranges, and you could explore them without suffering the thin air of high altitudes. Then we discovered the Forest Service's web page featuring a place called Snake Road, and my attitude changed from hopeful to intrigued.

Our first visit was in late summer. My parents and I drove slowly along the base of Pine Hills Bluff. The water level in the swamp was high on both sides of the road. We could only hope we weren't going to get stuck in the mud or even find ourselves up to the hubcaps in water. But were we actually going to see a snake? We had grave doubts. Then a long, black cylindrical creature zigzagged across the road: our first snake, and the first of many.

I know them now as North American Racers; back then they were just big impressive black mystery snakes. Snake Road lived up to its name: it was indeed a road with snakes. I couldn't have been more pleased. The snakes were enormous, at least to my North Dakota eyes. They looked as thick as my wrist (granted, I have narrow wrists), easily over 4 feet (1.2 meters) long, shiny black, and alert. And that was all it took. We saw many Northern Cottonmouths, but also Gray Ratsnakes, Western Ribbonsnakes, and even the occasional Timber Rattlesnake. We learned that many snakes, especially Northern Cottonmouths, crossed from the bluff to the swamp and back again each spring and fall. In short order, my years became divided into two phases: during the snake migration and preparing for the next snake migration.

For a place with so much biodiversity, Snake Road is surprisingly accessible. Those who aren't seasoned snake watchers should know that getting to where you can see snakes is often a hassle. Mud, water, thorny vegetation, biting insects, and uneven terrain are typical impediments. Enthusiasts put up with all of that because there usually isn't any other choice. But Snake Road is a maintained gravel road, which, despite the biting insects, takes much of the misery out of snake watching, while leaving the wonder intact.

When I first started visiting Snake Road, I couldn't tell a Northern Cottonmouth from an Eastern Copperhead, so I got myself a field guide. It was less than helpful. This is not a criticism of the field guide, but it wasn't what someone like me needed.

As a layperson, you can carefully match a photo from a field guide to a snake and *still* get the species identification wrong. It turns out—and this was a surprise to me when I first learned it—snakes of the same species can look different, and vary in color, and snakes of different species can look quite a bit alike. I was sure I found a Scarletsnake (*Cemophora coccinea*) about five years back, a gorgeous little critter. My friends were envious. Too bad it was really a juvenile Eastern Milksnake. A fine snake, to be sure, but not a Scarletsnake. I discovered my error when I pulled up a photograph to brag to a biologist friend that I had indeed seen a Scarletsnake at Snake Road. The one small photograph in my field guide *seemed* to match the animal I was looking at, and the range map indicated Scarletsnakes could be found here, but I still identified the species incorrectly. I don't blame the field guide. The problem was I didn't know enough about snakes to use it effectively. What I really needed was a guide designed for beginners. That guide was written for experts.

Field guides often expect you to capture and handle the snakes. For some species, the best way to identify them is to check markings on their bellies or count scales. It's illegal to handle the wildlife at Snake Road, so that's not an option. Moreover, even if handling were legal, there are three species of venomous snakes at Snake Road, and they make up well over half (65%) of the snakes I've observed there. If you're not sure what kind of snake you're looking at, you absolutely shouldn't touch it. Getting bitten is the worst way to determine if a snake is venomous.

For me and my growing Snake Road habit, the available field guides weren't the right tool for the job. I needed something to help me quickly identify, by sight alone, the snakes I was seeing in the field. Being an academic librarian, I enjoy digging into a good research problem, but there wasn't much out there about Snake Road apart from a couple of master's theses, which were technical and, frankly, above my head. Some investigation on the web turned up an article published in the *Bulletin of the Chicago Herpetological Society* (Palis, 2016) that listed the snake species that had been observed at Snake Road. That article gave me the list I needed, but I still didn't know how to identify the snakes on that list, which was my main goal. Luckily, shortly after that I met the article's author at Snake Road. We were both walking the same direction, so we chatted while we looked for snakes. Not knowing who I was talking to, I quoted his research back to him, which is a fine way to become acquainted with a researcher. We became friends. He taught me how to identify all the snakes that live there, and it was during one of our walks that I had the idea to write this book. I decided to take everything I had learned over the past few years and create a guide to the snakes of Snake Road to help aspiring snake watchers—people who are fascinated by snakes and want to learn but might not know where to start. And here it is, the book I wish someone could have given me when I first discovered Snake Road. I hope it will help you and the ones you love discover the joys of snake watching. Good luck and may all of your days be snaky!

Acknowledgments

This book and the field work it demanded would not have been possible without help. I am indebted first and foremost to the experts who reviewed drafts of this book and provided me with invaluable feedback. This book would not exist without your guidance, and I am deeply grateful. Thanks to Elisabeth Turner for accompanying me to Snake Road on many occasions and lending her sharp eyes to the task of snake spotting. I'm grateful to my parents, whose twice-yearly visits from North Dakota conveniently coincide with the spring and fall snaking seasons. Some families go to the beach together. We picnic and photograph pit vipers in southern Illinois. Thanks to my colleagues at Southern Illinois University and the staff of Morris Library, especially Susan Tulis. John Palis deserves special recognition; his comprehensive knowledge of Illinois herpetofauna is exceeded only by his patience and generosity. His article "Snakes of 'Snake Road'" inspired me to turn my hobby of photographing snakes into something worth sharing with others, and his support for this project was instrumental to its success. He even spotted my mudsnakes. Thanks to Shawn Gossman of hikingwithshawn.com, Mary Boehler, Jean Sellar, Erin Palmer, Becky Schneider, Christopher Smaga, Michael Deutsch, Jeremy Schumacher, Michael Dloogatch, Stephen Barten, John Archer, Ralph Shepstone, Gery Herrmann, and members of the Chicago Herpetological Society for walking the road with me and sharing your observations.

INTRODUCTION

Pine Hills Bluff, viewed from Winter's Pond. The crevices in the limestone bluff offer

What Is Snake Road?

Snake Road, also known as LaRue Road and Forest Road 345, is a 2.7-mile (4.3 kilometer) gravel road that is closed to automobiles twice each year—in fall and spring—but stays open to foot traffic year-round to protect snakes and other wildlife as they cross the road, some of them migrating to and from the limestone crevices of Pine Hills Bluff. Snake Road is located within the exceptionally biodiverse LaRue–Pine Hills–Otter Pond Research Natural Area.

Research Natural Areas, or RNAs, are designated by the federal government because they contain rare species, unique ecosystems, or other remarkable features that make them deserving of special and permanent protection. RNAs preserve biodiversity, maintain natural features, and provide a baseline to monitor long-term ecological change. RNAs are used to conduct scientific research and low-impact educational activities. Many RNAs, including the LaRue–Pine Hills–Otter Pond RNA, are managed by the US Forest Service, although the Illinois Department of Natural Resources has law enforcement authority to protect reptiles

snakes and other creatures protection from winter's chill.

and amphibians that live there. Snake Road enjoys the protections it does because of the RNA designation and the ongoing efforts of the US Forest Service and Illinois DNR.

It isn't just the migrating snakes that make Snake Road special. After all, only some of the species of snakes that you can observe there migrate, particularly Northern Cottonmouths, which typically make up most of the snake sightings. Rather, its location in southern Illinois places it at a unique ecological crossroad. You can observe species associated with the southern, northern, eastern, and western United States within walking distance of each other, sometimes interacting—or eating each other. Snake Road, Pine Hills Bluff, and LaRue Swamp are collectively known as the LaRue–Pine Hills, and the area is home to an astounding 23 species of snakes. Nowhere else in Illinois, and possibly the United States, can you observe so many different species in such a small, accessible location. Little surprise that snake watchers from all over the world travel to southern Illinois just to visit Snake Road.

The phrase "snake migration," while an accurate description of the event for some species, conjures vivid but misleading imagery. Snakes are neither herd nor flock animals. Unlike geese or other animals that migrate, snakes do not gather into enormous groups to migrate. A mother Timber Rattlesnake leaves a scent trail that her young follow back to the den before winter, but they don't move as a closely coordinated group. Different species might migrate at different times, and individuals of the same species might also migrate at different times. For convenience I refer to "migrations" or "the snake migration" as the periods in fall and spring when the US Forest Service closes Snake Road to automobiles, but that term isn't accurate, at least not when broadly applied. Many species of snakes at Snake Road don't migrate to and from the bluffs at all; they simply live in the area, and you can watch them going about their lives while the migratory species are migrating. This can give a visitor the erroneous impression that all the snake species are migrating, when only some are actually doing so. It might be more accurate to describe the periods in which the US Forest Service closes the road as the fall or spring snake-watching seasons.

Snake Road in early fall.

On Using This Book

This book is intended as a guide to visiting Snake Road, setting reasonable expectations, and visually identifying the snakes there. Snakes exhibit significant regional variation in appearance, even among individuals of the same species, so this guide is less useful the farther you go from Snake Road. Moreover, this region is at the edges of many species' ranges, so traveling just a few miles (3–5 kilometers) in any direction can change not just how some snakes look, but also what species of snakes you can see. Don't rely on this book anywhere outside of the LaRue–Pine Hills–Otter Pond Research Natural Area.

This book has two parts. Part 1 consists of 23 sections, one for each species of snake that has been observed at or near Snake Road. Each section includes photographs and descriptions to help you learn to recognize that species by sight. Part 2 compares visually similar species and suggests ways to tell them apart.

To help set reasonable expectations for your Snake Road visit, the 23 snakes have been organized into sections according to the probability you will encounter each species during a single 4-hour visit, starting with the Northern Cottonmouth, which you are almost certain to see, and ending with the Scarletsnake, which hasn't been seen in Illinois since 1942. Like any organizational scheme, this approach is imperfect. Snake watching is different for every person. Snakes' protective coloration can make them hard to spot, and some people are better at spotting camouflaged snakes than others. The weather, time of day, and time of year all affect snake behavior and your ability to notice them. Sometimes the snakes are nowhere to be seen. Sometimes you see a variety of species, and sometimes one particular species is visible in abundance. I once saw four Eastern Milksnakes during a single visit to Snake Road—a spectacularly unlikely event. Visiting Snake Road is a little like gambling, and I suspect it's that same intermittent positive reinforcement (fun, exciting discoveries occur, but on a random schedule) that keeps so many of us coming back. You never know what you're going to see.

Setting Your Expectations

The key to an enjoyable visit to Snake Road is reasonable expectations. Long before I started working on this book, I met a Norwegian couple at Snake Road on a particularly pleasant and snaky spring day. They had traveled from Norway just to visit Snake Road and were in a noticeably crummy mood, which surprised me because I was having a perfectly excellent day of snake watching.

"We have only seen 37 snakes today," they complained.

I'm sure I looked confused, and they explained they thought the snake migration would be spectacular, with hundreds or even thousands of snakes crossing the road at once. They should have been thrilled to see 37 snakes, which is a solid count for a walk down Snake Road, but instead they left disappointed. Their expectations were simply unrealistic, and it ruined their visit.

To find out what realistic snake-watching expectations should be, I did what I'm sure any perfectly reasonable person would do: I spent three years conducting an observational study. During that time, I visited Snake Road on 100 occasions (35 in 2017, 39 in 2018, and 26 in 2019), spent a total of 380.75 hours there, and observed 1,716 snakes. I learned that the answers to three questions can help set reasonable expectations for a visit to Snake Road:

1. How many snakes and how many species can I expect to see?
2. What is the probability of seeing each species?
3. What time of year should I visit?

How many snakes and how many species can I expect to see?

On average, for each hour you spend at Snake Road in spring or fall, you can expect to observe 4 snakes and 1 species. If you visit Snake Road for three or four hours on a typical day, which is roughly the amount of time it takes to walk the length of Snake Road from gate to gate and back again, you could expect to see 12 to 16 snakes of 3 to 4 species. But not all days are typical, and some days I saw a lot of species diversity. In 18 percent of my visits, I observed 7 or more species, and on one very special day I observed 11 species. Sometimes I saw a lot of snakes. In 11 percent of my visits, I observed snakes at a rate of 10 per hour or higher. On my all-time snakiest day, I observed snakes at the rate of 27 snakes per hour. I was spotting a snake almost every two minutes and reached a total of 163 (133 were Northern Cottonmouths). And sometimes—thankfully not often—there just isn't much going on. In 3 percent of my visits, I observed only 1 snake, and on one occasion I observed no snakes whatsoever. If you want to see a lot of snakes, and especially if you want to see a variety of species, I recommend planning multiple visits and walking Snake Road for at least four hours per visit. And if you stay longer, you'll probably see more.

Northern Cottonmouths will probably account for most of your snake observations. During my study period, I observed more Northern Cottonmouths (1,072) than all other species of snakes combined (644), although the majority of the Northern Cottonmouth observations were in fall. See the chart for the number of snakes I observed per hour by season. The light green bar represents the number of Northern Cottonmouths per hour, and the dark green bar represents all other species per hour.

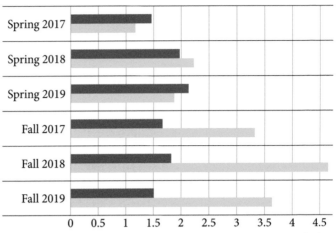

Snakes per hour, by season. Light green = Northern Cottonmouths; green = all other species.

Regardless of season, I always observed far more Northern Cottonmouths than any other species of snake, and it was only in spring 2017 and spring 2019 that hourly observations of the 22 other species of snakes combined managed to exceed Northern Cottonmouths. On any given visit to Snake Road, there's a small chance you won't see a single snake. But if you do, expect to see at least one Northern Cottonmouth, possibly many Northern Cottonmouths, and perhaps nothing but Northern Cottonmouths.

What is the probability of seeing each species?

Some of the 23 snake species that have been documented at or near Snake Road might actually be more numerous than others. Other species behave in a way that makes spotting one of them rare. Red-bellied Mudsnakes might be abundant, but they're highly aquatic and seldom move onto the road. I saw an average of one Red-bellied Mudsnake for every 190 hours I spent walking Snake Road. If you want to spot a seldom-seen snake, plan multiple visits and spend as much time there as you can. To estimate the probability of seeing each species, I tabulated the number of visits in which I observed at least one individual of that species, as well as the two species I failed to observe.

Total snakes observed by species, number of visits, and probability

Species	Individuals observed	Visits (n = 100) in which at least one individual was observed	Probability of observing at least one individual during a visit (%)
Northern Cottonmouth	1,072	90	90
Plain-bellied Watersnake	167	67	67
Western Ribbonsnake	77	43	43
Ring-necked Snake	78	40	40
Rough Greensnake	59	35	35
Gray Ratsnake	57	33	33
Dekay's Brownsnake	38	25	25
North American Racer	38	22	22
Mississippi Green Watersnake	29	20	20
Eastern Copperhead	21	17	17
Timber Rattlesnake	21	17	17
Red-bellied Snake	16	12	12
Smooth Earthsnake	11	9	9
Common Gartersnake	11	8	8
Eastern Black Kingsnake	6	5	5
Common Wormsnake	5	5	5
Eastern Milksnake	2	2	Negligible
Diamond-backed Watersnake	2	2	Negligible
Red-bellied Mudsnake	2	2	Negligible
Eastern Hog-nosed Snake	2	2	Negligible
Flat-headed Snake	2	0	Negligible
Common Watersnake	0	0	Negligible
Scarletsnake	0	0	Negligible

For example, I observed Eastern Copperheads on 17 out of 100 visits, or 17 percent of visits. Think of your probability like rolling a die with 100 sides each time you visit. If you roll that die and you get a 17 or below, you see an Eastern Copperhead. Roll an 18 or above and you don't. Visit the road again and the probability of seeing an Eastern Copperhead on that visit remains 17 percent. With more visits your probability of seeing an Eastern Copperhead goes up, but only because you get to keep rolling that die. You break 50 percent only after four visits, meaning you could visit four times and still be as likely to see an Eastern Copperhead as not. You'd have to visit Snake Road 25 times to raise your probability of seeing an Eastern Copperhead to 99 percent, and even then, you could still fail to see one. During my trips to Snake Road between 2017 and 2019, I failed to see two species from the list of species previous observed there, the Common Watersnake and Scarletsnake, so their probabilities are given as negligible. Four other species, the Diamond-backed Watersnake, Eastern Milksnake, Red-bellied Mudsnake, and Flat-headed Snake, I only saw twice, so their probabilities are also given as negligible.

When should I visit if I want to see the most snakes?

During my 100 visits to Snake Road during spring and fall, my observations seemed to follow a pattern. In spring, I observed few snakes until late March or mid-April when the numbers peaked, then tapered off for the remainder of the season. Snake observations per hour gradually increased throughout the autumn and peaked in late October or early November. You can't plan your visits to coincide with the peaks because they vary from year to year. To be there for a peak, you will need to come often, get lucky, or both. If you can come for only one day and want to maximize your chance of picking a snaky day, choose a day in mid-April or mid-October. Late autumn is the better time to see the most snakes.

The charts reflect the snakes I observed per hour and give you a sense of when you might want to visit to see the most snakes, but there were some more granular differences between my spring and fall observations that are worth sharing. As you can see in the three tables, I observed 9 species of snakes at comparable rates in spring and fall, 6 species of snakes more frequently in spring, and 6 species of snakes more frequently in fall. And by more frequently, I mean at least twice as often, sometimes much more often.

What are the limitations of this study?

My visits to Snake Road varied in several ways, all of which could have affected the number of snakes I observed.

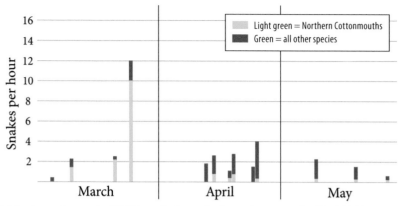

Total snakes per hour, spring 2017. The peak of my snake observations occurred on March 24. My visit on March 26 yielded no snake observations, so there is no bar representing it on this chart.

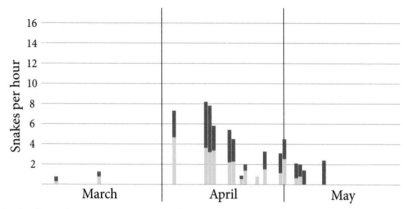

Total snakes per hour, spring 2018. The peak of my snake observations occurred on April 11.

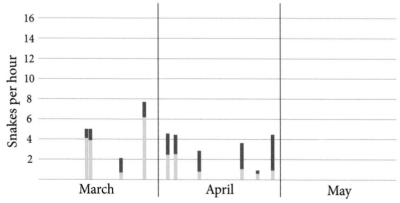

Total snakes per hour, spring 2019. The peak of my snake observations occurred on March 28.

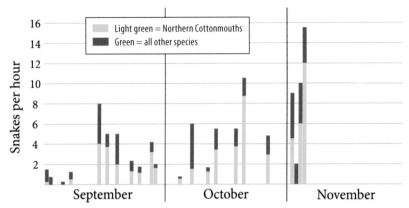

Total snakes per hour, fall 2017. The peak of my snake observations occurred on November 5.

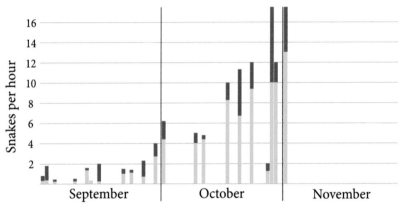

Total snakes per hour, fall 2018. The peak of my snake observations occurred on October 30.

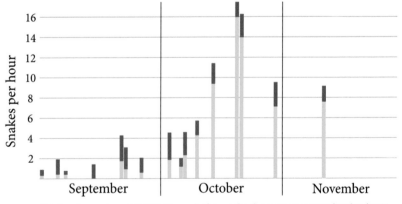

Total snakes per hour, fall 2019. The peak of my snake observations occurred on October 21.

The six species of snakes I observed more frequently in spring

Species	Hours per snake observed (2017–19)	
	Spring	Fall
Ring-necked Snake	2.91	11.01
Red-bellied Snake	13.19	69.75
Smooth Earthsnake	17.15	209.25
Common Gartersnake	19.05	104.63
Eastern Black Kingsnake	28.58	None observed
Common Wormsnake	34.30	None observed

The six species of snakes I observed more frequently in fall

Species	Hours per snake observed (2017–19)	
	Spring	Fall
Northern Cottonmouth	0.60	0.27
Rough Greensnake	12.25	4.65
Mississippi Green Watersnake	34.30	8.72
Timber Rattlesnake	171.50	10.46
Eastern Milksnake	None observed	104.63
Red-bellied Mudsnake	None observed	104.63

The nine species of snakes I observed at comparable rates in both spring and fall

Species	Hours per snake observed (2017–19)	
	Spring	Fall
Plain-bellied Watersnake	2.32	2.25
Western Ribbonsnake	6.60	4.10
Gray Ratsnake	5.04	9.10
Dekay's Brownsnake	7.80	13.08
North American Racer	10.09	9.96
Eastern Copperhead	21.44	16.10
Flat-headed Snake	171.50	209.25
Diamond-backed Watersnake	171.50	209.25
Eastern Hog-nosed Snake	171.50	209.25

Sometimes I walked with one or more companions whose skill at snake spotting varied. When joined by experienced snake watchers, I probably observed more snakes. When joined by an inexperienced person, I probably saw fewer snakes because my attention was divided between looking for snakes and making sure my companion didn't step on a Northern Cottonmouth.

The timing of visits was determined by my job duties and the weather. As a result, sometimes I visited Snake Road three or four days in a row, sometimes every other day, and other times I didn't visit for over two weeks. The path I took on each visit varied. Some walks began at the north end of the road and some at the south. Sometimes I walked halfway and turned around. Trips varied in duration, most often lasting three and a half to four hours, but sometimes only two to three hours, and on a few occasions, seven hours or more.

It is important that you recognize my study for what is was: one snake enthusiast's observations, shared in the hope of helping future visitors to Snake Road establish reasonable expectations and have the best snake-watching experience they possibly can.

Preparing to Visit Snake Road

Now that your expectations have been primed, I have a few suggestions for maximizing the quality of your visit to Snake Road.

Walk in the afternoon. Snakes can be observed throughout the day and night, but cool mornings don't often yield many snake observations. Because of the height of the bluffs and shade from trees, Snake Road doesn't get much direct sunlight until around noon. I start consistently spotting snakes only after the sun has been up for several hours. In my experience, noon until just after sunset is generally the most productive time to visit.

Put safety first. Venomous snake bites are rare, but serious. Indeed, I have heard of only two venomous snake bites at Snake Road. Both bites were from baby Northern Cottonmouths, both to photographers. And in both cases, as the stories go, these people were bitten by one snake while photographing a different snake. It wasn't the snake they saw that bit them; it was the snake they didn't see. Before you sit, squat, or lie down at Snake Road, carefully inspect the area around you. For every snake you see, there are untold numbers of snakes you don't. And even though snake bites are rare, it's good to have a plan for what to do if someone in your party gets bitten. I carry a fully charged mobile phone with the number for poison control (800-222-1222) and the address and number for the nearest hospital, St. Joseph Memorial Hospital in Murphysboro, Illinois: 2 Hospital Drive, Murphysboro, Illinois, 62966. Their telephone number is 618-684-3156. If I were bitten, I would immediately start walking back to my car while calling 911. I would also remove any jewelry or tight clothing that might become uncomfortable if the area swells and to make sure medical professionals will have easy access. That's my plan. Your plan should be unique to you and your party's specific needs.

Walk slowly. Don't imagine that you will be able to see snakes, even large ones, from much farther away than 10 feet (3 meters). Sometimes the road can seem clear ahead, only to reveal a Northern Cottonmouth when you're about to step on it. Many of the snakes of Snake Road are very small, with full-grown adults not much over a foot (0.3 meters) long. These little snakes can be difficult to see from even 3 feet (1 meter) away. They can see you coming and might even feel your footsteps from a distance, and they tend to freeze when they sense danger, making them hard to spot unless you look directly at them. The slower you go, the more snakes you're likely to see.

Divvy up responsibility for searching. If you come with friends, have one person scan the road itself, one person scan the right shoulder and vegetation, and one person scan the left shoulder and vegetation.

Juvenile Smooth Earthsnake with penny for scale.

Snakes can be anywhere, from under a fallen leaf at your feet to far above the ground on a branch. I once watched a group walk right past a gorgeous 4-foot (1.2 meter) Timber Rattlesnake without noticing it. The snake was coiled up in a patch of sunlight just off the side of the road, as obvious as an animal with protective coloration can be, but they were all looking straight ahead.

Visit more than once. Snake activity is difficult to predict. You can show up on a sunny mid-October day and not see a single snake even though the conditions seem ideal and the date is close to when the peak of fall snake activity seems to occur. Or you can visit, as I did, on a chilly and rainy 45-degree (7.2 Celsius) day in late February, expecting a damp and snakeless walk, only to encounter Northern Cottonmouths at a rate of more than one per minute. Best to make peace with the notion that some days will be snaky, some days will be snakeless. If you want to ensure you see snakes, plan multiple visits. If you're visiting from far away, I strongly recommend staying two or three days if you can manage it. Southern Illinois is replete with good food and comfortable lodging. You won't suffer.

Carry plenty of water. For a full-length walk up and down Snake Road, I like to carry 2 liters of water for myself. On warmer days, sometimes I run out. A Snake Road visit can get uncomfortable if you're thirsty, and there's nowhere nearby to find clean drinking water.

Wear comfortable shoes or boots. In hiking terms, Snake Road is an easy walk, but 5.4 miles (8.7 kilometers) of Snake Road's large and irregular gravel can be miserable in sandals or soft shoes. You could be walking for hours, so make sure your footwear is up to the challenge.

Protect yourself from the sun. Walking Snake Road end to end takes roughly four hours. Four hours of hiking means four hours of sunlight, especially on the top of your head and neck. Despite the shade from the bluffs, it's easy to get a sunburn. I recommend a wide-brimmed hat and plenty of sunscreen. A hat does more than just protect you from the sun: you'll see more snakes if you're not squinting.

Stay on the road. It's easy enough to accidentally step on a Northern Cottonmouth or another critter while walking on a flat gravel road. If you leave the road, you'll face more hazards. Poison ivy is just about everywhere. The woods are full of ticks and mosquitos. You could step on a venomous snake concealed by a clump of vegetation or its own protective coloration. There are lots of holes, vines, and loose rocks just waiting to turn an ankle. From a conservation perspective, human presence near the bluffs disrupts habitat and increases erosion, slowly destroying this place that so many of us love. And in the spring, some Northern Cottonmouths literally fall off the edge of the bluff, sometimes dropping 50 feet (15 meters) or more onto the ground below. The chances of being directly underneath a falling Northern Cottonmouth are very low, but not zero. Falling rocks, however, are more dangerous than falling snakes, and you're more likely to be hit with one of them if you leave the road.

Prevent insect and tick bites. Snake Road is adjacent to a mosquito factory called LaRue Swamp, and ticks in this region can carry a variety of unpleasant and debilitating infections. To keep mosquitos and their ilk away, I apply insect repellent containing DEET to my outerwear immediately before each walk. To keep the ticks away, I soak every garment I wear to Snake Road in permethrin (a readily available insecticide) twice each season. Permethrin goes on wet, but after it dries it persists in the fabric for weeks, even through multiple washes. I've found it to be remarkably effective, although you should always perform a full body tick check after each visit.

Carry binoculars. These can help you surveil the road ahead of you and see snakes before they see you. They're surprisingly handy, especially for spotting critters out in the swamp that you'd otherwise miss.

Pack a flashlight. This can be useful for peering into holes and crevices, but also because Snake Road gets dark rather fast after sunset. I consider my flashlight one of my most critical pieces of equipment and always carry spare batteries.

Part of being properly equipped for a visit to Snake Road is knowing what *not* to bring. Snake Road is subject to rules, both formal and informal, that might be unfamiliar to you. Being familiar with these rules could save you from dirty looks, injury, or legal prosecution.

Snake hook, tongs, or other equipment for handling wildlife. Snake Road has been plagued by poachers illegally collecting snakes for the pet trade. It is illegal to handle, herd, or harass snakes at Snake Road. If you are in possession of a hook or tongs, law enforcement treats it as intent to collect, and that carries stiff penalties.

Pillowcases or any container that could be used to transport captive snakes. Even if you aren't transporting snakes, you can be prosecuted for simply possessing such a container at Snake Road.

Pets. Your fellow snake watchers will be furious with you if your dog scares away a snake they were admiring. It's also way too easy for the animal to blunder into poison ivy, ticks, or a venomous snake.

Alcoholic beverages. Snake Road is the most accessible and safe place I know of to go snake watching, provided you take appropriate precautions. It might seem obvious, but venomous snakes and alcohol are a terrible combination. People under the influence of alcohol are dramatically more likely than a sober person to harass, touch, or hold a venomous snake, and get bitten. Don't drink or let your friends drink before or during a visit to Snake Road. Do yourself a favor and enjoy a beer or one of our local wines *after* the visit.

Snakebite kit. They just don't work. Suction devices have been shown to be ineffective at removing venom, and some kits include a scalpel for making an incision at the bite site. Do not use it. Cutting someone after they've been bitten is adding injury to injury. If you or anyone in your party gets bitten, seek medical attention immediately.

Travel Information

Snake Road runs north and south and is accessible from both ends. The north entrance, off Muddy Levee Road, can be a bumpy ride but has the most parking. It accommodates roughly 15 vehicles. There are also picnic tables with grills and a garbage barrel.

The south entrance, off LaRue Road, has minimal parking and no amenities. Perhaps five cars can comfortably fit in the small parking area, although it's possible to parallel park

Map of Illinois. Snake Road is in southwestern Illinois, just north of the town of Wolf Lake.

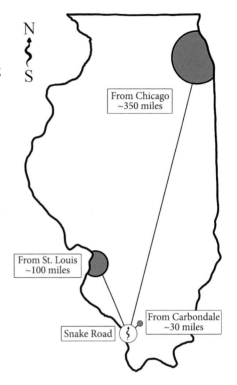

along the sides of the road leading up to the south entrance. Please note that there are no restrooms at either entrance and no access to drinking water.

Traveling south on Highway 3

To reach the north entrance. As you are traveling south toward Wolf Lake, watch for a bridge crossing the Big Muddy River. Note that when heading south, if you've reached Wolf Lake you've passed Snake Road.

Immediately after crossing the bridge, turn left on Muddy Levee Road. A word of caution: Muddy Levee Road is a loose gravel road, and you need to slow down in order to spot it and turn onto it at a safe speed. Signal your left turn and start to slow down as you get to the middle of the bridge. After making the turn, follow Muddy Levee Road until it reaches a T at the base of Pine Hills Bluff, 2.7 miles (4.3 kilometers). Drive slowly, and watch for potholes and snakes, both of which can be hard to see before you hit them. Turn right at the T in the road. The parking lot for Snake Road is on your right after about 150 yards (~137 meters). Take the final approach slowly and watch for pedestrians and critters. I found a lovely Eastern Milksnake basking in the middle of the road right before the parking lot and would have run it over if I hadn't been driving slowly and watching carefully.

To reach the south entrance. On Highway 3, continue over the Big Muddy River and drive another 1.3 miles (2 kilometers). Turn left on LaRue Road and follow it until you reach the gate to Snake Road, about 1.2 miles (1.9 kilometers). The road curves to your left. Drive slowly and remain alert

Pine Hills Bluff near the north entrance to Snake Road.

for that last mile. You can often see snakes crossing or basking on this stretch of road.

Traveling north on Highway 3

To reach the south entrance. After passing through the town of Wolf Lake, go another 2.8 miles (4.5 kilometers) and turn right on LaRue Road. Follow it until you reach the gate to Snake Road, about 1.2 miles (1.9 kilometers). The road curves to your left as you approach the south gate to Snake Road. Drive slowly and remain alert for that last mile. You can often see snakes crossing or basking on this stretch of road.

To reach the north entrance. After passing through Wolf Lake, go another 4 miles (6.4 kilometers) north and turn right on Muddy Levee Road immediately before the bridge over the Big Muddy River. Slow down significantly before turning. Muddy Levee Road is gravel, and it can be easy to lose control of your vehicle on this turn. Watch for potholes and mud on Muddy Levee Road. Follow Muddy Levee Road until it reaches a T at the base of Pine Hills Bluff, about 2.7 miles (4.3 kilometers), and then turn right. The parking lot for Snake Road is on your right after about 150 yards (~137 meters).

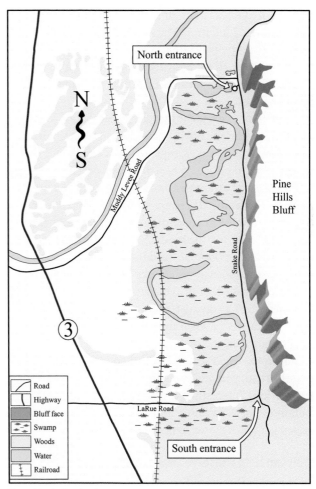

North entrance

N
S

Muddy Levee Road

Pine
Hills
Bluff

Snake Road

③

| Road |
| Highway |
| Bluff face |
| Swamp |
| Woods |
| Water |
| Railroad |

LaRue Road

South entrance

Map of Snake Road and vicinity.

Rules of the Road

Once you've arrived at Snake Road, you need to be aware of some laws and matters of etiquette.

Never handle or touch snakes or other animals. It's terribly tempting to grab a beautiful or unusual snake, but resist the urge. Snake Road is located within a Research Natural Area and handling is illegal.

Always allow snakes to go where they want. Preventing a snake from going somewhere or encouraging it to move in a specific direction is called "herding" and is illegal.

Replace lifted logs, rocks, or other cover objects. If you move anything to look for critters hiding under it, always carefully return it to its original position. This is good for the animals that dwell underneath them, but it's also the law. Leaving rocks or logs overturned disrupts the habitat and harms the wildlife.

Travel by foot. Leave your bicycles, motorbikes, scooters, and any other wheeled conveyances (except wheelchairs) at home. Wheels kill snakes, especially the small ones that you're less likely to notice. Wheelchairs are welcome at Snake Road, but please be aware that not all parts of Snake Road are wheelchair friendly. There are stretches covered with large, jagged gravel, and depending on the season, shallow pools of water covering the road. Occasionally there will be deadfall obstructing the road, and there are some substantial potholes. If you choose to visit Snake Road using a wheelchair, please do your best to avoid running over any critters, because they won't always get out of the way. Many reptiles and amphibians freeze when they sense danger, and that can be lethal if they're in the path of a wheel.

Be courteous. Don't scare away someone else's find. While walking the road, you might see someone ahead of you looking at something interesting. If you want to see what the fuss is about, move forward slowly and quietly and ask permission before you get much closer than 15 feet (4.5 meters).

How You Can Help Conserve Snake Road

One of the main threats to Snake Road comes from those of us who visit it. Some people who go snake watching shift groundcover to find critters that might be hiding underneath. Rolling logs and turning over stones, however, damages habitat that requires weeks or months to properly recover. You can do your part by always returning logs and stones you lift exactly to their original positions. It's not just the right thing to do, it's the law. You can be prosecuted for failing to return cover items to their original location.

Better yet, when visiting Snake Road, skip looking under cover objects entirely. In my many visits, I've noticed that logs and stones along Snake Road are shifted frequently, sometimes a dozen or more times per day, disrupting the microhabitats under them and driving away whatever might have been living there. Every single species of snake at Snake Road can be seen on the road itself, so you might as well save yourself some effort—and give the habitat a much-needed break—and leave the cover items in place.

Handling snakes is also a threat to the ecosystem, which is part of why it is illegal at Snake Road. You can inadvertently introduce new pathogens to the area or spread existing pathogens from an infected animal to a healthy one. Handling snakes can be dangerous for people, too. Even if you are certain the snake you're reaching for is nonvenomous, you might not see the Northern Cottonmouth next to it.

To protect Snake Road and places like it for future generations of snake watchers, researchers, and for the snakes themselves, carefully replace objects you look under, refrain from handling the animals, and, if you have friends who might be ambivalent about snakes, bring them with you. The best protection for snakes everywhere is education. The more people understand snakes, the less they'll fear them.

A Note on Names

One of the purposes of this book is to help visitors to Snake Road identify the snakes they encounter and learn their names. This goal seems straightforward, but in reality it is deceptively complicated. As science progresses, sometimes scientific names change to reflect new knowledge. Not all scientists agree, however, resulting in controversy over some of these new names. This is a normal, healthy part of the scientific process. But it makes coming up with a definitive list of species names darn near impossible. For simplicity's sake I only included species-level English and scientific names, and I drew those names from the list maintained by the Society for the Study of Amphibians and Reptiles.

A Note on the Photography

The photographs in this book were selected from more than 30,000 images I took over a period of three years, almost entirely at or in the vicinity of Snake Road. The Scarletsnake photos were taken by contributing photographers. I used two cameras, a speedlight, and three lenses. I used Sony a7ii and

Top, venomous snake enthusiast taking a photograph of a Northern Cottonmouth. *Below*, Red-bellied Mudsnake.

Sony a7Riii cameras and a Sony FE 90mm macro lens, a Zeiss Batis 25mm wide-angle lens, and a Sony FE 100–400mm telephoto lens. The 90mm macro served as my primary lens, and I recommend that focal length as the sweet spot for anyone aspiring to serious snake photography at Snake Road. Shorter lenses demand that you get uncomfortably close to your subject, and longer lenses work poorly in the low-light conditions common on Snake Road.

Snake photographers commonly manipulate the snakes they wish to photograph and coax them into satisfactory poses. While I empathize with the impulse, especially with rarely observed species, I find that you get the best photographs of snakes going about their business without human interference. The technical term for this is "in situ" (Latin for "where it is"), and it's my standard operating procedure. This hands-off approach means sometimes only getting two or three shots of a snake before it flees, but it yields photographs that I believe are most true to the nature of the snake. And at Snake Road handling snakes is illegal, so in situ photography keeps you on the right side of the law.

On Visually Identifying Snakes

Handling snakes at Snake Road is illegal, so you must identify them by sight alone. This can make identification challenging, but that's part of the cost of preserving this exceptional natural resource. Fortunately, it is possible and, really, not that difficult to learn to visually identify all 23 species of snakes that you might observe at Snake Road.

For the purposes of this book I use three broad size categories to describe snakes: large, medium, and small. Large snakes exceed 4 feet (1.3 meters) in length when fully grown. Medium snakes reach between 3 and 4 feet (0.9 to 1.3 meters) in length when fully grown. Small snakes are less than 3 feet (1 meter) in length when fully grown, and six snakes in this category don't even reach 18 inches (0.4 meters).

Keep in mind that even within the same species, snakes vary in size tremendously throughout their lifespans. A young North American Racer is not much larger than a pencil, while a healthy adult could exceed 6 feet (2 meters). Except in special cases, size isn't an especially useful factor in identifying snakes. I'm only including these broad size categories to give you a general sense of how large or small these animals are when fully grown. As you walk the road, keep in mind that although snakes come in a wide range of sizes, most of the snakes you're likely to see will be less than 3 feet (1 meter) long and quite a few will be 16 inches (0.4 meters) or shorter. A baby Smooth Earthsnake might be only a few inches (8–10 centimeters) long. Curled up, it can hide under a coin. Just because a snake is small, however, doesn't mean it's young.

Visually identifying snakes is complicated by a few other factors. Some species look different when they're young, and not just because they're smaller than adults. Northern Cottonmouths (see page 30), Plain-bellied Watersnakes (see page 36), Gray Ratsnakes (see page 51), North American Racers (see page 58), and Common Watersnakes (see page 105) all have young that exhibit colors and patterns quite unlike the adults of those species. For each of these species I have provided images of young animals as well as adults.

Some species come in multiple color schemes, or variants, not unlike how automobile manufacturers offer the same car in different paint jobs. Smooth Earthsnakes (see page 78), Eastern Hog-nosed Snakes (see page 98), Dekay's Brownsnakes (see page 55), Red-bellied Snakes (see page 74), and Gray Ratsnakes (see page 51) have one or more distinct variants. But keep in mind that individuals of every species of snake, not just the ones listed here, can vary. When possible, I have included photographs with examples of these variations.

Left, adult North American Racers are black or bluish black with pale noses. *Right*, unlike adults, baby North American Racers are covered with brown blotches over a creamy white background. This pattern fades with age.

Snakes have two kinds of scales: keeled and smooth. Keeled scales have a ridge running down the length of each scale, like the keel on the bottom of a boat. Keels can be strong, meaning they have a pronounced ridge down the middle, or light, with a slight ridge down the middle. Smooth scales have no keel. Whether the scales are keeled, and to what degree, can be key to identifying a snake.

Snakes of the same species can vary in color, size, and pattern, so it is unwise to rely on any single

Left, keeled scales. These belong to a Timber Rattlesnake. Snakes with keeled scales sometimes have "rough" in their English names, which gives us names like Rough Greensnake. *Right*, smooth scales. These belong to a Red-bellied Mudsnake. Snakes with smooth scales sometimes have "smooth" in their English names, which gives us names like Smooth Earthsnake.

characteristic—especially color—when identifying a snake. Look for multiple characteristics.

Eastern Copperheads (see page 65) do indeed occur at Snake Road, but that snake you might think is an Eastern Copperhead is probably a young Northern Cottonmouth (see page 30). Unless it really is an Eastern Copperhead. To learn more, see the section on telling the difference between Northern Cottonmouths and Eastern Copperheads (see page 117). Until you're familiar with snake identification, it can be easy to mistake some of the more similar species. Species that are from the same genus, such as Northern Cottonmouths and Eastern Copperheads, can be particularly challenging at first. To help with that problem, section 2 of this book is devoted to illustrating the differences between commonly confused species.

Finally, bear in mind that a single photograph is worth a thousand dimly recalled details. When taking photographs for the purpose of future identification, try to get the side of the snake's head in good focus. Lip scales and their markings can be useful for determining species.

1. Northern Cottonmouth (Venomous)

Scientific name	*Agkistrodon piscivorus*
Size	Medium
Cottonmouth ratio	1:1
Appearance of young	Young appear different from adults
Probability of seeing one	1 visit, 90%; 4 visits, 99%; 10 visits, >99%

If you see only one species of snake at Snake Road, it will probably be a Northern Cottonmouth. When you approach a Northern Cottonmouth, it tends to freeze and hold its mouth open, revealing the white interior that gives it its English name. This behavior is called "gaping." It is a defensive posture meant to discourage potential predators. Sometimes a Northern Cottonmouth will inflate its body, widen the head, and shake the tip of its tail. Although these behaviors can seem threatening, Northern Cottonmouths don't typically bite except when harassed.

Maintain a respectful distance of no less than 4 feet (1.2 meters) when you're observing Northern Cottonmouths at Snake Road. If a snake feels threatened, it might flee to safety, which, from the snake's perspective, could be behind

Like the other two venomous snakes of Snake Road, Northern Cottonmouths are pit vipers. They have a heat-sensing pit on each side of the head between the eye and the nostril.

Northern Cottonmouths can vary in color. Some, like this one, are brown and tan.

Some Northern Cottonmouths are very dark, with little or no visible pattern on their backs.

Some Northern Cottonmouths retain their bands into adulthood. These markings can be especially noticeable when the animal is wet.

Left, Northern Cottonmouths have keeled scales. *Right*, when sensing danger, or just to get a better view of the surroundings, Northern Cottonmouths tilt their heads at a 90-degree angle from the body, revealing their checkered chins.

Northern Cottonmouths can often be found resting or basking on Snake Road. Be careful not to step on one.

Northern Cottonmouths are frequently seen in and near water, and for good reason. Their scientific name translates as "hook-toothed fish-eater."

Left, when alarmed, Northern Cottonmouths gape, revealing the white interior of the mouth. If a Northern Cottonmouth is gaping, you're too close. *Right*, some Northern Cottonmouths emerge from the swamp coated in green duckweed.

Left, this Northern Cottonmouth just had a swim, leaving it clean and shiny. *Right*, when Northern Cottonmouths and other snakes flick their tongues, they're tasting the air.

Baby Northern Cottonmouths are shaped like small adults. They are lighter in color, however, with more pronounced banding, so they are routinely mistaken for Eastern Copperheads (see page 65).

Late summer and fall are when baby Northern Cottonmouths are born. Around that time there can be quite a few of them on Snake Road.

you. Make sure you leave the snake a clear path to the woods or the water and give yourself space to get out of the way if the snake decides to move.

Similar to Plain-bellied Watersnake (see page 36), Eastern Copperhead (see page 65), Diamond-backed Watersnake (see page 93), Common Watersnake (see page 105), and Mississippi Green Watersnake (see page 62).

How to tell apart from Plain-bellied Watersnakes (see page 114), Eastern Copperhead (see page 117), and black snakes (see page 112).

For more information on Northern Cottonmouths, see Ernst and Ernst (p. 481), Gibbons (p. 307), Phillips et al. (p. 264), Powell et al. (p. 437).

The tip of a baby Northern Cottonmouth's tail is pale green or yellow, which fades with age. Young Eastern Copperheads share this characteristic.

As they mature, baby Northern Cottonmouths grow darker and their bands usually fade.

Left, baby Northern Cottonmouths are usually around a foot (0.3 meters) in length. *Right*, baby Northern Cottonmouths vary in color. Many are brown and tan, but some have brick-red markings on their heads.

2. Plain-bellied Watersnake

Scientific name	*Nerodia erythrogaster*
Size	Large
Cottonmouth ratio	6:1
Appearance of young	Young appear different from adults
Probability of seeing one	1 visit, 67%; 4 visits, 98%; 10 visits, >99%

Once you've seen the belly of a Plain-bellied Watersnake, the species seems misnamed. While their backs are indeed rather plain and typically gray or black, these snakes have richly colored bellies, usually vivid yellow or orange. In this case, the word "plain" refers not to color, but to the lack of the distinctive markings found on the bellies of other species of watersnakes. Plain-bellied Watersnakes tend to be wary and energetic. When confronted with a threat, they might freeze or flee, but sometimes they posture. Like a cat raising its fur, Plain-bellied Watersnakes alter their silhouettes. The head becomes triangular, the neck narrows, and the body flattens out or inflates. Together, these changes seem to mimic the appearance of a Northern Cottonmouth.

Left, although they are drab when viewed from above, Plain-bellied Watersnakes have brightly colored bellies. *Right*, their bellies aren't a single solid color all the way down. Toward the middle of the body, the belly scales have dark markings that resemble the rungs of a ladder.

Left, this Plain-bellied Watersnake froze in place rather than posturing defensively. Note how the head is not much wider than the neck. *Right*, plain-bellied Watersnake in a defensive posture. The head is flexed to appear triangular, and the body is inflated. If you see a Plain-bellied Watersnake acting like this, you're probably too close.

If you're not seeing any Plain-bellied Watersnakes on the road, look for them basking on branches above the swamp.

Left, you can find Plain-bellied Watersnakes all over the Snake Road area, even far from water. *Right*, Plain-bellied Watersnakes have heavily keeled scales.

The contrasting brown-and-black pattern of young Plain-bellied Watersnakes differs noticeably from adults, whose patterns have become faded and are often imperceptible.

This young adult Plain-bellied Watersnake has lost most of its juvenile pattern. Only a few faint bands remain.

Juvenile and adult Plain-bellied Watersnakes have dark orange bars on the margins of their lip scales.

Close-up view of a Plain-bellied Watersnake's juvenile pattern.

Similar to Northern Cottonmouth (see page 30), Gray Ratsnake (see page 51), North American Racer (see page 58), Mississippi Green Watersnake (see page 62), Diamond-backed Watersnake (see page 93), and Common Watersnake (see page 105).

How to tell apart from Northern Cottonmouth (see page 114) and black snakes (see page 112).

For more information on Plain-bellied Watersnakes, see Ernst and Ernst (p. 242), Gibbons (p. 264), Phillips et al. (p. 226), Powell et al. (p. 416).

3. Western Ribbonsnake

Scientific name	*Thamnophis proximus*
Size	Small
Cottonmouth ratio	14:1
Appearance of young	Young resemble smaller adults
Probability of seeing one	1 visit, 43%; 4 visits, 89%; 10 visits, 99%

Despite the three bright stripes running down the body, Western Ribbonsnakes blend into their surroundings better than you might expect. They sometimes freeze when sensing danger, but they usually flee when approached. If you spot one, appreciate it from where you stand. You might never get closer than when you first noticed it.

Western Ribbonsnakes are tolerant of low temperatures, so you can see them throughout the year, even on days too cold for most other snakes. They are routinely confused with their heavier-bodied cousin, the Common Gartersnake, which also sports three yellow stripes, but Western Ribbonsnakes are far more frequently encountered at Snake Road.

The lip scales above the mouth are pale cream or white.

Western Ribbonsnakes have keeled scales and three orange or yellow stripes. The top stripe is usually orange, and the side stripes are typically pale yellow. But don't rely on those characteristics. Sometimes all three stripes will be pale yellow.

Western Ribbonsnakes have plain, cream-colored bellies.

Capable climbers, Western Ribbonsnakes can be seen in bushes, on tree branches, or even on the face of the bluff.

Despite the flamboyant coloration, a motionless Western Ribbonsnake can be difficult to spot from a distance.

On cool but sunny days, look for Western Ribbonsnakes basking in bushes or on low tree branches.

Similar to Common Gartersnake (see page 81).

How to tell apart from Common Gartersnakes (see page 126).

For more information on Western Ribbonsnakes, see Ernst and Ernst (p. 405), Gibbons (p. 141), Phillips et al. (p. 250), Powell et al. (p. 428).

4. Ring-necked Snake

Scientific name	*Diadophis punctatus*
Size	Small
Cottonmouth ratio	14:1
Appearance of young	Young resemble smaller adults
Probability of seeing one	1 visit, 40%; 4 visits, 87%; 10 visits, 99%

Ring-necked Snakes are often not much larger than a pencil, so they blend into the sticks and leaves on Snake Road quite well. Their coloration ranges from bluish black to gray to brown, but all Ring-necked Snakes have a narrow yellow or orange band around the neck, which gives the species its English name. If you look closely—and you should—the scales are iridescent. These little snakes are an excellent reason to walk slowly and to watch your step. They usually freeze when sensing danger and are easy to miss. Their babies are especially tiny, just a few inches (~8 centimeters) long and not much thicker than a match.

Left, the bright yellow or orange ring around the neck usually has a dark border.
Right, Ring-necked Snakes have smooth scales and, in strong light, are iridescent.

Left, in soft light Ring-necked Snakes appear dark brown, gray, or black. *Right*, these diminutive snakes can be spotted resting, stretched out, or coiled up in shady spots on Snake Road.

You can find Ring-necked Snakes at any time of day, but during the hottest hours they tend to be found in areas of deep shade.

The rings on Ring-necked Snakes can be faint and dull or rich and bright, and they range in color from yellow to orange. The rings, which usually take the form of a slightly uneven band about two scales thick, can vary in size and shape as well. Notice the unusual widow's peak of orange extending down the middle of this snake's back.

Left, some Ring-necked Snakes are mostly brown. *Right*, some Ring-necked Snakes are mostly gray.

Similar to Red-bellied Snake (see page 74) and Common Wormsnake (see page 87).

How to tell apart from black snakes (see page 112).

For more information on Ring-necked Snakes, see Ernst and Ernst (p. 90), Gibbons (p. 106), Phillips et al. (p. 202), Powell et al. (p. 403).

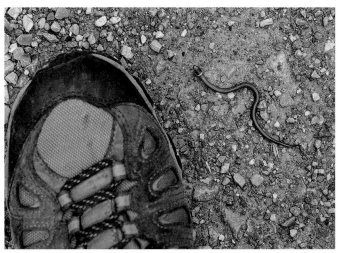

Ring-necked Snakes are quite small, especially their young. The author's boot is included for comparison.

This baby Ring-necked Snake is so small it could hide under a quarter. If you want to see the most snakes, make sure to keep an eye out for snakes of all sizes, not just the big ones.

5. Rough Greensnake

Scientific name	*Opheodrys aestivus*
Size	Small
Cottonmouth ratio	18:1
Appearance of young	Young resemble smaller adults
Probability of seeing one	1 visit, 35%; 4 visits, 82%; 10 visits, 98%

A living vine, the Rough Greensnake is one of Snake Road's most difficult snakes to spot, but it's the easiest to identify with its long, slender body and emerald green coloring. If you see a bright green snake, without a doubt, it's a Rough Greensnake. Excellent climbers, Rough Greensnakes spend much of their time in bushes and trees where they are nearly invisible. They reinforce this camouflage by moving with a slightly swaying motion, like a vine caught in a soft breeze. To increase your chances of spotting one of these beautiful snakes, don't just watch the road. Be sure to scan bushes and branches at shoulder level and below.

Left, Rough Greensnakes have a vividly green back that fades to a light green, yellow, or white belly. *Right*, Rough Greensnakes are called "rough" because their scales are keeled, meaning each scale has a ridge running down the center.

Rough Greensnakes are never easy to spot while they are climbing, but on windless days their gentle swaying motion can reveal them.

Adult Rough Greensnakes can be around 3 feet (1 meter) long, but their bodies are very slender.

Protective coloration makes Rough Greensnakes hard to spot amid green vegetation.

A young Rough Greensnake looks like a small adult, but it has a disproportionately large head and eyes.

There are no other bright green snakes at Snake Road, so a long, slender green snake will always be a Rough Greensnake.

For more information on Rough Greensnakes, see Ernst and Ernst (p. 258), Gibbons (p. 117), Phillips et al. (p. 234), Powell et al. (p. 382).

6. Gray Ratsnake

Scientific name	*Pantherophis spiloides*
Size	Large
Cottonmouth ratio	19:1
Appearance of young	Young appear different from adults
Probability of seeing one	1 visit, 33%; 4 visits, 79%; 10 visits, 98%

Visitors to Snake Road rapidly become acquainted with the game of stick or snake. From a distance, it's hard to tell one from the other, so when you see something long and dark on the road, you're constantly guessing whether it's a stick or a snake. Adult Gray Ratsnakes are long. Many exceed 5 feet (1.5 meters) and often bask stretched out rather than coiled up. They are known for kinking themselves every few inches (5–10 centimeters), disrupting the outline of their bodies, which makes it even more difficult to determine if they are a stick or snake. North American Racers and Ring-necked Snakes also display this behavior, so kinking doesn't necessarily indicate a Gray Ratsnake. Excellent climbers, Gray Ratsnakes can be seen resting in the safety of the branches of a tree, or clinging to the side of the bluff, seeming to defy

Adult Gray Ratsnakes can grow quite long. It's not unusual to encounter one that is 5 feet (1.5 meters) long or longer.

Left, most Gray Ratsnakes at Snake Road have entirely black backs. *Right*, some Gray Ratsnakes are covered with light blotches.

Left, Gray Ratsnakes have black bars on the margins of the lip scales. On this animal, the bars are ragged and pronounced. *Right*, bars on the margins of the lip scales can vary from individual to individual. On this animal, the bars are comparatively faint.

Above left, Gray Ratsnakes have white chins and necks. *Right*, although Gray Ratsnakes have white chins and necks, the belly is darker and interrupted with light splotches.

Gray Ratsnakes have lightly keeled scales.

Left, a Gray Ratsnake displaying obfuscatory kinking. On Snake Road, this behavior makes them easy to mistake for a stick or branch. *Above right*, baby Gray Ratsnakes look different from adults. They are covered with strongly contrasting dark blotches on a light background. These blotches range in color from brown to black.

gravity. Adult Gray Ratsnakes at Snake Road are usually entirely black on the back and sides, but a few are black with gray blotches.

Similar to Plain-bellied Watersnake (see page 36), North American Racer (see page 58), and Eastern Hog-nosed Snake (black variant) (see page 98).

How to tell apart from North American Racers (see page 121) and black snakes (see page 112).

For more information on Gray Ratsnakes, see Ernst and Ernst (p. 115), Gibbons (p. 192), Phillips et al. (p. 206), Powell et al. (p. 388).

A baby Gray Ratsnake with nearly black blotches.

As Gray Ratsnakes mature, the light background usually fades to black.

7. Dekay's Brownsnake

Scientific name	*Storeria dekayi*
Size	Small
Cottonmouth ratio	38:1
Appearance of young	Young resemble smaller adults
Probability of seeing one	1 visit, 25%; 4 visits, 68%; 10 visits, 94%

Dekay's Brownsnakes, named after the zoologist who discovered the species, come in an array of shades and colors and are among the most variable snakes of Snake Road. Some are dark brown, which obscures the stripes and spots that run the length of the body. Some are tan with white accents. I even saw one that was brick red. These diminutive snakes usually freeze when approached, but a few will coil and strike. Don't be alarmed. They're too small to pose a risk to anything larger than an earthworm. Just back away and give them their space. Dekay's Brownsnakes can often be seen basking or resting in wheel ruts on Snake Road, which makes them easy to spot (if you're looking for minuscule snakes), but also vulnerable to being run over during the times of the year when the road is open to automobiles.

Dekay's Brownsnakes often have a pale stripe running down the middle of the back, sometimes interrupted by brown bars or spots.

Dekay's Brownsnakes have one or two dark spots or triangles below each eye.

Similar to Red-bellied Snake (see page 74), Smooth Earthsnake (see page 78), and Flat-headed Snake (see page 102).

How to tell apart from Red-bellied Snakes (see page 124).

For more information on Dekay's Brownsnakes, see Ernst and Ernst (p. 327), Gibbons (p. 61), Phillips et al. (p. 244), Powell et al. (p. 423).

Left, some Dekay's Brownsnakes have dark brown oblong spots on each side of the neck, just behind the mouth. *Right*, Dekay's Brownsnakes vary in color, from pale tan to dark brown.

Left, Dekay's Brownsnakes are fairly tolerant of the cold and can be seen basking on Snake Road on cool and sunny days early in spring and late in fall. I've even seen them out in early February. *Right*, Dekay's Brownsnakes are small enough to hide under fallen leaves, and you can easily step on them if you're not careful.

Dekay's Brownsnakes have keeled scales.

8. North American Racer

Scientific name	*Coluber constrictor*
Size	Large
Cottonmouth ratio	28:1
Appearance of young	Young appear different from adults
Probability of seeing one	1 visit, 22%; 4 visits, 62%; 10 visits, 91%

This snake's English name serves as an accurate description. North American Racers are fast and alert, and they often flee at the first sign of danger. North American Racers are not a snake you often see up close. On hot days when most other snakes are hidden away, you can find North American Racers basking in direct sunlight. The hotter it is, the better. They are capable climbers, so pay attention to bushes and trees while you walk. The snake you're looking for might be above you. If you get lucky enough to observe one up close, you might notice the scales on their flanks sometimes have an iridescent blue sheen.

North American Racers have large eyes and prominent nostrils.

Check sunlit and elevated spots on the sides of Snake Road for basking North American Racers.

This climbing North American Racer offers a glimpse of its white belly.

A North American Racer periscoping. North American Racers and other snakes sometimes raise the front of the body into the air, affording an elevated view of their surroundings.

North American Racers have smooth scales.

Adult North American Racers are large, extremely alert snakes.

Baby North American Racers are covered with brown and orange spots on a white background. When they move, those spots blur together, making the snakes hard to follow with your eyes.

Above left, apart from the enormous eyes, baby North American Racers hardly resemble adults. *Right*, as they grow, North American Racers gradually lose their juvenile pattern.

Similar to Plain-bellied Watersnake (see page 36), Gray Ratsnake (see page 51), and Eastern Hog-nosed Snake (black variant) (see page 98).

How to tell apart from the Gray Ratsnake (see page 121) and black snakes (see page 112).

For more information on North American Racers, see Ernst and Ernst (p. 77), Gibbons (p. 212), Phillips et al. (p. 200), Powell et al. (p. 369).

9. Mississippi Green Watersnake

Scientific name	*Nerodia cyclopion*
Size	Medium
Cottonmouth ratio	37:1
Appearance of young	Young resemble smaller adults
Probability of seeing one	1 visit, 20%; 4 visits, 59%; 10 visits, 89%

Judging from the name, you might expect Mississippi Green Watersnakes to be bright green snakes, but their coloration actually ranges from dark green to yellowish brown to olive drab. Like other watersnakes, Mississippi Green Watersnakes are semiaquatic and can be observed basking on the shore or perched on a branch above a watery escape route. While not unusual at Snake Road, Mississippi Green Watersnakes are a threatened species found almost nowhere else in Illinois. They typically remain motionless when you approach them, provided you don't get too close. Although this snake can be seen throughout the year, I've encountered them most often in late fall.

You can identify Mississippi Green Watersnakes by the tiny scale separating the bottom of the eye from the top of a lip scale. No other snakes at Snake Road have such a scale.

Because of the banding along the sides, Mississippi Green Watersnakes can be difficult to tell apart from Diamond-backed Watersnakes, especially from a distance.

Sometimes the banding will be only faintly visible.

Similar to Northern Cottonmouth (see page 30), Diamond-backed Watersnake (see page 93), Common Watersnake (see page 105), and Plain-bellied Watersnake (see page 36).

How to tell apart from Diamond-backed Watersnakes (see page 132).

For more information on Mississippi Green Watersnakes, see Ernst and Ernst (p. 219), Gibbons (p. 281), Phillips et al. (p. 224), Powell et al. (p. 415).

When approached, Mississippi Green Watersnakes tend to freeze rather than flee or posture. The drab coloration and lack of movement make this snake easy to miss even if you're standing next to one.

Mississippi Green Watersnakes have strongly keeled scales.

10. Eastern Copperhead (Venomous)

Scientific name	*Agkistrodon contortrix*
Size	Medium
Cottonmouth ratio	51:1
Appearance of young	Young resemble smaller adults but with yellow tip to the tail
Probability of seeing one	1 visit, 17%; 4 visits, 52%; 10 visits, 84%

Eastern Copperheads have some of the most effective protective coloration of any snake at Snake Road, at least as far as human beings are concerned. You might walk within a foot (0.3 meters) of one and never notice it. While many snakes have bands, an Eastern Copperhead's bands usually have a distinct shape that can help you identify them. They are narrow at the top of the snake's back and widen as they approach the belly. If a snake you suspect of being an Eastern Copperhead is small, under 18 inches (0.7 meters) long or so, make sure it's not a young Northern Cottonmouth. Young Eastern Copperheads and Northern Cottonmouths are probably the two most frequently confused species of snakes at Snake Road.

Left, this Eastern Copperhead gives us a good view of its chin, which is creamy white and lightly speckled, with a thin dark stripe running along each side of the mouth. *Right*, Eastern Copperhead coloration ranges from a warm, leafy brown to rusty orange, but these colors become dull as the time to shed approaches.

Eastern Copperheads, like many snakes, can sometimes be seen climbing trees, vines, and even the bluff face. Unknowingly, I passed within 6 inches (15 centimeters) of this animal.

Eastern Copperheads often freeze when sensing a disturbance, and their protective coloration makes them easy to miss.

This Eastern Copperhead almost vanishes on a bed of leaf litter. Look away for a moment and it can be hard to find it again.

Baby Eastern Copperheads are born in the late summer or fall and resemble small adults, except for the yellow tips of their tails.

Protective coloration isn't always effective. On a gravel road or away from fallen leaves, Eastern Copperheads tend to stand out.

Eastern Copperheads have keeled scales.

Similar to Northern Cottonmouth (see page 30), Common Watersnake (see page 105), and Eastern Milksnake (see page 90).

How to tell apart from Northern Cottonmouths (see page 117).

For more information on Eastern Copperheads, see Ernst and Ernst (p. 473), Gibbons (p. 302), Phillips et al. (p. 262), Powell et al. (p. 436).

11. Timber Rattlesnake (Venomous)

Scientific name	*Crotalus horridus*
Size	Large
Cottonmouth ratio	51:1
Appearance of young	Young resemble smaller adults
Probability of seeing one	1 visit, 17%; 4 visits, 52%; 10 visits, 84%

Sadly, Timber Rattlesnakes have endured many decades of human persecution. Today this magnificent animal is threatened in Illinois and sightings at Snake Road are rare. Most of my sightings have been of young snakes or snakes that have recently eaten. Being ectotherms, Timber Rattlesnakes require warmth to help digest their food, and a rattlesnake in a sunbeam is much easier to spot than a rattlesnake hiding under a log. If you are fortunate enough to see an adult Timber Rattlesnake, there's a chance you're only seeing it because it has a full belly and needs to digest. To confirm that, look for a lump toward the middle or back third of the snake. It's always a good idea to keep your distance from a Timber Rattlesnake, but if it has a meal in its belly, give the snake an especially wide berth of at least 10 feet (3 meters) and don't follow it if it moves. A fed snake is a vulnerable snake. When alarmed, a snake that has recently eaten will sometimes vomit up its meal to facilitate escape. Timber Rattlesnakes need nutrition in the fall to survive winter's fast and in the spring to regain energy, so the loss of a meal could potentially be life threatening.

Young Timber Rattlesnakes grow quickly, shedding their skin perhaps three times every two years, but this slows down as they age. Shedding happens as a result of growth, and growth happens over time and with successful hunting. Each time a Timber Rattlesnake sheds, it gains a segment at the base of its rattle. Rattles are made of the same material as your fingernails, and in the wild they routinely break off. Consequently, there is no way to definitively calculate a rattlesnake's age by counting the segments on a rattle. Rough estimates are all we get. Two Timber Rattlesnakes from the same clutch might not hunt with equal success, and as a result, they might end up with a different number of segments in their rattles.

If you succeed in spotting a Timber Rattlesnake, please refrain from sharing your discovery on social media, or if you do, wait at least a week before posting anything. In the aftermath of Timber Rattlesnake sightings shared on social media, I've observed small hordes of snake watchers and snake haters descending on an area, some hoping for a glimpse or photograph, others looking to capture or kill the animal. Either way, this is not good for the snake.

Timber Rattlesnakes are threatened in the state of Illinois. If you see one, be careful not to disturb it. Appreciate it from a distance and move along.

Left, Timber Rattlesnakes have a broad, triangular head and elliptical pupils. Never rely on either of these characteristics to identify a snake, though. They can be misleading (some snakes can change the shape of their heads to appear triangular, and elliptical pupils can appear round in dim light conditions). Those characteristics can vary and result in false positives or false negatives if you rely upon them exclusively. Also, observing them requires you to get far too close. *Right*, Timber Rattlesnakes are pit vipers. You can see a heat-sensitive pit between the eye and the nostril.

While only rattlesnakes grow rattles, many species of snakes vibrate their tails when alarmed.

Left, Timber Rattlesnakes at Snake Road are predominantly gray with a gold stripe running down the center of the back. *Above*, Timber Rattlesnakes tend to move slowly, but they're always alert. This snake is periscoping, or raising up its neck and head to get an elevated view of its surroundings.

Spot the Timber Rattlesnake. Their protective coloration can be remarkably effective.

Newborn Timber Rattlesnakes are roughly a foot long (0.3 meters) and resemble small adults.

Baby Timber Rattlesnakes are born with a rattle that has only one segment, called a button.

This Timber Rattlesnake's recent meal shows up as a bulge, expanding its body so much you can see the white skin between the scales.

Timber Rattlesnakes are capable climbers. If you want to see one, don't forget to check the trees.

Similar to Eastern Hog-nosed Snakes (spotted variant) (see page 98).

For more information on Timber Rattlesnakes, see Ernst and Ernst (p. 503), Gibbons (p. 322), Phillips et al. (p. 268), Powell et al. (p. 440).

12. Red-bellied Snake

Scientific name	*Storeria occipitomaculata*
Size	Small
Cottonmouth ratio	67:1
Appearance of young	Young resemble smaller adults
Probability of seeing one	1 visit, 12%; 4 visits, 40%; 10 visits, 72%

Of all the snakes at Snake Road, Red-bellied Snakes vary the most in appearance. I enjoy their variations, but it also makes them easy to misidentify. The body can be gray, brown, yellow, or a combination of colors. The head can be rust red, black, or gray, and will often be mottled. There is usually a light yellow spot on the back of the neck, sometimes flanked by smaller spots on either side. Sometimes the spots merge, giving the appearance of a ring. If you see a snake with a clearly defined ring around its neck, it will be a Red-bellied Snake or a Ring-necked Snake (see page 44).

Many Red-bellied Snakes resemble the animal in the photo at the beginning of this section. The body is light brown or yellowish, the head is rust red with black and gray mottling, and there is a light yellow spot where the head meets the body. Every Red-bellied Snake has a single white scale on the upper lip, just behind and below the eye. No other snake at Snake Road has a white scale there—if you see that scale, you've found a Red-bellied Snake.

The name is something of a misnomer. Red-bellied Snakes at Snake Road have bellies that vary in color and can be salmon, yellow, orange, or even white. I've never seen one

Left, probably the single most reliable characteristic for identifying Red-bellied Snakes is the bright white scale on the top lip, just behind and below the eye. *Right*, even though this snake's coloration is unusual, the telltale white scale stands out.

Left, Red-bellied Snakes often have light spots on the back and sides of the neck, although these spots vary, as the following photos show. *Right*, sometimes the spots are only faintly visible.

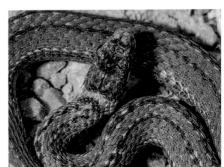

Left, sometimes the spots are distinct. *Right*, sometimes the spots on the back and sides of the head merge into a collar.

Above, don't rely on color to identify Red-bellied Snakes. Instead, look for the spot on the back of the head and especially the white scale below and behind the eye. *Right*, this Red-bellied Snake is mostly yellow.

This Red-bellied Snake is mostly gray.

This Red-bellied Snake has the more typical rust-red head, but its neck spots have merged into a collar and its body is brown and gray.

with a red belly, but since handling snakes at Snake Road is illegal, I can only see their bellies when they lift their heads up, and that doesn't happen especially often.

Similar to Ring-necked Snake (see page 44) and Dekay's Brownsnake (see page 55).

How to tell apart from Dekay's Brownsnakes (see page 124).

For more information on Red-bellied Snakes, see Ernst and Ernst (p. 333), Gibbons (p. 65), Phillips et al. (p. 246), Powell et al. (p. 424).

This Red-bellied Snake has rust-red stripes on its back and sides.

Left, this Red-bellied Snake is gray with orange and black stripes on its back. *Right*, Red-bellied Snakes have keeled scales.

13. Smooth Earthsnake

Scientific name	*Virginia valeriae*
Size	Small
Cottonmouth ratio	97:1
Appearance of young	Young resemble smaller adults
Probability of seeing one	1 visit, 9%; 4 visits, 31%; 10 visits, 61%

Smooth Earthsnakes tend to be either brown or gray. Their drab coloration contrasts with their smooth, glossy scales that shimmer in bright light. Their large eyes stand out as a dominant feature. Smooth Earthsnakes are easy to miss unless you walk slowly and stay alert. Be especially careful when walking through fallen leaves: there could be a Smooth Earthsnake beneath one. Like many of the other especially small snakes at Snake Road, Smooth Earthsnakes can be found throughout the day, but they favor shady areas while the sun is high. I've seen most of my Smooth Earthsnakes late in the afternoon, within about two hours of sunset.

Smooth Earthsnakes are very small, making them difficult to spot. Adults might be the size of a fat pencil, while babies can hide underneath a coin.

Smooth Earthsnakes have eyes that are comparatively large for their heads.

Smooth Earthsnakes come in two variants: brown and gray. This is an example of the gray variant.

Brown variants, like this one, seem to be much more common than gray variants.

Perhaps gray variants seem less common because they blend into the road better.

Above, Smooth Earthsnakes have smooth scales. *Right*, you're more likely to see Smooth Earthsnakes later in the afternoon and into the night.

Similar to Dekay's Brownsnake (see page 55), Common Wormsnake (see page 87), and Flat-headed Snake (see page 102).

How to tell apart from Flat-headed Snakes (see page 128) and Common Wormsnakes (see page 130).

For more information on Smooth Earthsnakes, see Ernst and Ernst (p. 448), Gibbons (p. 53), Phillips et al. (p. 260), Powell et al. (p. 412).

14. Common Gartersnake

Scientific name:	*Thamnophis sirtalis*
Size:	Small
Cottonmouth ratio:	97:1
Appearance of young:	Young resemble smaller adults
Probability of seeing one:	1 visit, 8%; 4 visits, 28%; 10 visits, 56%

Abundant throughout much of the United States, Common Gartersnakes are an unusual sight on Snake Road. Named after an antique article of clothing known for its bright stripes, the garter, this poor animal has had its name abused perhaps more than any other North American snake. A garter is a thin band of brightly colored fabric used to hold up socks or leg coverings that was made obsolete by the invention of elastic. As garters fell out of use, this once straightforward and descriptive name became obscure and was replaced by similar-sounding names that made sense to people who had never used a garter, such as "garden snake" or "gardener snake." For those interested in language change, this phenomenon is called an eggcorn. Tolerant of

Left, the coloration of Common Gartersnakes varies. There are always three light stripes and two dark stripes down the back, but some individuals also have red spots along the sides. *Right*, some lack the red spots.

Left, Common Gartersnakes have keeled scales. *Right*, sometimes the dark stripes along the back are almost solid black.

Sometimes the dark stripes along the back are checkered with pairs of white bars.

low temperatures, Common Gartersnakes can be observed on days too cold for most other snakes.

//

Similar to Western Ribbonsnake (see page 40).

How to tell apart from Western Ribbonsnakes (see page 126).

For more information on Common Gartersnakes, see Ernst and Ernst (p. 424), Gibbons (p. 128), Phillips et al. (p. 256), Powell et al. (p. 431).

Common Gartersnakes usually have three or more black bars on the margins of their upper lip scales, but these bars sometimes only extend halfway down each scale.

After a rain, look for Common Gartersnakes basking in the branches of bushes or small trees. Since it's not legal to handle snakes at Snake Road, finding them in bushes and trees is one of the few ways to see their bellies, which are plain except for spots running along the edges.

15. Eastern Black Kingsnake

Scientific name	*Lampropeltis nigra*
Size	Medium
Cottonmouth ratio	179:1
Appearance of young	Young resemble smaller adults
Probability of seeing one	1 visit, 5%; 4 visits, 18%; 10 visits, 40%

Their black and white coloration lends Eastern Black Kingsnakes a dramatic appearance. If you spot one of these handsome, speckled snakes, be sure to move slowly and lightly on your feet if you're hoping for a closer look. They tend to be wary and often flee when approached. Eastern Black Kingsnakes at Snake Road don't seem to vary much in appearance. Their bodies are black, covered with white or cream-colored speckles of various sizes. Some individuals sport rows of closely spaced speckles that resemble subtle bands across the top of the back.

Distinctive, speckled black-and-white (or cream) coloring makes Eastern Black Kingsnakes easy to identify. Nothing else at Snake Road looks quite like them.

Eastern Black Kingsnakes have cream-colored bellies interrupted by gray or black checks.

Left, Eastern Black Kingsnakes at Snake Road are covered in speckles that are smaller at the top of the back and larger near the belly. *Right*, unlike other black snakes at Snake Road, Eastern Black Kingsnakes have cream-colored spots on the top of the head.

Similar to Gray Ratsnake (see page 51) and North American Racer (see page 58).

How to tell apart from black snakes (see page 112).

For more information on Eastern Black Kingsnakes, see Ernst and Ernst (p. 167), Gibbons (p. 173), Phillips et al. (p. 218), Powell et al. (p. 379).

Young Eastern Black Kingsnakes look like small adults.

Eastern Black Kingsnakes have smooth scales.

16. Common Wormsnake

Scientific name	*Carphophis amoenus*
Size	Small
Cottonmouth ratio	214:1
Appearance of young	Young resemble smaller adults
Probability of seeing one	1 visit, 5%; 4 visits, 18%; 10 visits, 40%

Common Wormsnakes are seldom seen during the day, but when you see them in direct sunlight, these burrowing snakes are magnificently iridescent. They range in color from gray to brown (sometimes with a purple cast that photographs don't capture). The orange, salmon, or peach color of the belly extends almost halfway up the sides, making them one of the few snakes at Snake Road whose belly color you can see without handling them. Its English name is appropriate. I've heard several people ask if it's a worm when they saw one for the first time. Wormsnakes are typically found beneath logs and rocks, but they can sometimes be seen on Snake Road around dusk or after dark.

Left, Common Wormsnakes vary in color from silvery gray to shades of brown. *Right*, in direct sun or other strong light, their scales are iridescent.

Above, the belly color extends about a third of the way up the snake's side. *Right*, when ready to shed, Common Wormsnakes appear pale and almost milky.

Common Wormsnakes are very small. This juvenile was about 6 inches (15 centimeters) long.

This Common Wormsnake is light brown with a peach-colored belly.

Common Wormsnakes have smooth scales and small, uniformly black eyes. Their mouths are nearly invisible.

Similar to Ring-necked Snake (see page 44) and Smooth Earthsnake (see page 78).

How to tell apart from Smooth Earthsnakes (see page 130).

For more information on Common Wormsnakes, see Ernst and Ernst (p. 53), Gibbons (p. 79), Phillips et al. (p. 194), Powell et al. (p. 401).

17. Eastern Milksnake

Scientific name	*Lampropeltis triangulum*
Size	Small
Cottonmouth ratio	500+:1
Appearance of young	Young resemble smaller adults
Probability of seeing one	Negligible

Despite their dramatic coloration, Eastern Milksnakes can blend into their surroundings surprisingly well.

Because of their beautiful coloration, Eastern Milksnakes are one of the three most sought-after snakes at Snake Road, along with Red-bellied Mudsnakes and Timber Rattlesnakes. Alas, like those other two snakes, the probability of encountering an Eastern Milksnake is low. All you can do is put in the time walking the road and keep your snake eyes open. Eastern Milksnakes tend to freeze when sensing danger, making them hard to spot if they're not resting in a wheel rut or somewhere exposed. Young Eastern Milksnakes are easily mistaken for Scarletsnakes (see page 108).

The orange or red blotches on Eastern Milksnakes are ringed by uneven black borders.

Left, an Eastern Milksnake's head is only slightly wider than the neck, and the eyes are usually the same orange or red as the body. *Right*, young Eastern Milksnakes resemble adults, although their blotches tend to be red, which fades to orange as they mature.

Eastern Milksnakes have smooth scales.

Similar to Eastern Copperhead (see page 65), Common Watersnake (see page 105), and Scarletsnake (see page 108).

How to tell apart from Scarletsnakes (see page 138).

For more information on Eastern Milksnakes, see Ernst and Ernst (p. 176), Gibbons (p. 162), Phillips et al. (p. 220), Powell et al. (p. 381).

18. Diamond-backed Watersnake

Scientific name	*Nerodia rhombifer*
Size	Large
Cottonmouth ratio	500+:1
Appearance of young	Young resemble smaller adults but with stronger pattern
Probability of seeing one	Negligible

These large semiaquatic snakes are almost never seen on or around Snake Road. While it's possible Diamond-backed Watersnakes are rare in the LaRue–Pine Hills area, it seems more likely that their habits simply make them difficult to observe. Diamond-backed Watersnakes don't overwinter in the bluffs, so they have no need to cross the road in the spring or fall. They typically remain close to water, and you can see them basking on branches above the swamp or on partially submerged logs. With so much brush concealing the shorelines along Snake Road, though, it would be easy for one of these wary snakes to slip into the water unnoticed when someone approaches.

Diamond-backed Watersnakes can sometimes be seen basking on branches above the water.

Left, Diamond-backed Watersnakes have orange eyes and dark bars on the margins of their lip scales. *Right*, like Plain-bellied and Common Watersnakes, Diamond-backed Watersnakes can make their heads appear triangular as part of a defensive posture.

Diamond-backed Watersnakes have strongly keeled scales.

This Diamond-backed Watersnake has well-defined bands. On some individuals, however, the bands will be quite faint.

This snake has been basking long enough to dry out, and its bands are hardly visible.

Similar to Northern Cottonmouth (see page 30), Plain-bellied Watersnake (see page 36), Mississippi Green Watersnake (see page 62), and Common Watersnake (see page 105).

How to tell apart from Mississippi Green Watersnakes (see page 132).

For more information on Diamond-backed Watersnakes, see Ernst and Ernst (p. 242), Gibbons (p. 273), Phillips et al. (p. 230), Powell et al. (p. 419).

19. Red-bellied Mudsnake

Scientific name:	*Farancia abacura*
Size	Medium
Cottonmouth ratio	500+:1
Appearance of young	Young resemble smaller adults but with more vivid coloration
Probability of seeing one	Negligible

The Red-bellied Mudsnake is Snake Road's crown jewel. The iridescent black scales and vividly colored belly make this elusive snake a sight to behold. Highly aquatic, Red-bellied Mudsnakes are probably the most desired but least-seen snakes at Snake Road. If you travel to Snake Road with the explicit goal of seeing one, understand that your chance of seeing a Red-bellied Mudsnake is probably not any higher there than anywhere else in its range. Unfortunately for snake watchers, Red-bellied Mudsnakes don't overwinter in the bluffs, giving them no need to cross Snake Road during the spring or fall. Regular visitors to Snake Road report seeing as few as one or two per decade. In five years of walking Snake Road (over 150 visits and counting), I've seen two.

Left, Red-bellied Mudsnakes are seldom observed at Snake Road, but the few sightings I know about all happened near the swamp. *Right*, Red-bellied Mudsnakes have smooth, iridescent scales.

Left, the red of the belly extends onto the sides in regularly spaced patches, almost like waves. *Right*, Red-bellied Mudsnakes will hide their heads under a coil of the body.

How to tell apart from black snakes (see page 112).

For more information on Red-bellied Mudsnakes, see Ernst and Ernst (p. 126), Gibbons (p. 284), Phillips et al. (p. 210), Powell et al. (p. 405).

20. Eastern Hog-nosed Snake

Scientific name	*Heterodon platirhinos*
Size	Medium
Cottonmouth ratio	500+:1
Appearance of young	Young resemble smaller adults with spots
Probability of seeing one	Negligible

Eastern Hog-nosed Snakes are famous for their elaborate defensive behaviors. When alarmed, these snakes can inflate the body, hiss, spread the loose skin around the neck like a cobra, or strike with a closed mouth. They will even roll over and open their mouths, playing dead. Eastern Hog-nosed Snakes have two main variants at Snake Road: black and spotted. The black variants sometimes exhibit faint light circles or splotches on the back, and sometimes they're almost entirely black or dark gray. The spotted variants can be predominantly brown or gray with yellow spots, which on some individuals can be bright yellow—a truly remarkably snake to behold. Regardless of coloration, look for the distinctive upturned nose to make a positive identification.

Eastern Hog-nosed Snakes are very rarely observed at Snake Road, and if you do see one, it can be easy to mistake for another species. Black variants are easily mistaken for Plain-bellied Watersnakes or Northern Cottonmouths. The spotted variant, which can be predominantly brown, gray, or even bright yellow, is sometimes mistaken for a Timber Rattlesnake.

A spotted variant Eastern Hog-nosed Snake. The yellow spots on this animal are somewhat muted.

This black variant has faint spotting.

Left, Eastern Hog-nosed Snakes use their unique snouts to unearth buried toads and other subterranean delicacies. *Right*, from above, an Eastern Hog-nosed Snake in a defensive posture can have an almost cobra-like appearance.

When sensing danger, Eastern Hog-nosed Snakes can flatten the head and spread the loose skin around the neck. This individual looks quite fierce indeed.

An Eastern Hog-nosed Snake not displaying defensive posturing. Compare this image to the previous one. The shape of the head can change dramatically.

Eastern Hog-nosed Snakes have keeled scales.

As a defensive measure, Eastern Hog-nosed Snakes will roll upside down, defecate, and open the mouth (sometimes sticking out the tongue) in a ploy to appear dead and unappetizing to a potential predator.

Similar to Northern Cottonmouth (see page 30), Timber Rattlesnake (see page 69), North American Racer (see page 58), Gray Ratsnake (see page 51), and Plain-bellied Watersnake (see page 36).

How to tell apart from black snakes (see page 112).

For more information on the Eastern Hog-nosed Snake, see Ernst and Ernst (p. 146), Gibbons (p. 145), Phillips et al. (p. 214), Powell et al. (p. 408).

21. Flat-headed Snake

Scientific name:	*Tantilla gracilis*
Size:	Small
Cottonmouth ratio:	500+:1
Appearance of young:	Young resemble smaller adults
Probability of seeing one:	Negligible

From a distance, diminutive Flat-headed Snakes appear somewhat drab. They're just little brown snakes. Up close, however, their beauty is revealed. Their scales are a warm golden brown, and in direct sunlight they shine with iridescence. Much of the ground around Snake Road consists of a mix of rocks, dirt, fallen leaves, and decaying wood, riddled with gaps and crannies, and Flat-headed Snakes are excellent burrowers. Seeing a Flat-headed Snake burrow is like watching a watersnake slip into a pool, except Flat-headed Snakes disappear into ground that looks and feels solid. It's almost magical. A subtle serpent indeed, Flat-headed Snakes are seldom spotted on Snake Road.

Flat-headed Snakes can quickly burrow into loose, rocky ground.

The head tends to be, but isn't always, darker than the body, which is golden brown or tan.

As the time to shed draws near, the darker coloration on the head becomes faint and the eyes appear cloudy.

Flat-headed Snakes have smooth, glossy scales that grow darker toward the edges.

Flat-headed Snakes have a wedge-shaped head and small, uniformly black eyes.

Similar to Smooth Earthsnake (see page 78), Red-bellied Snake (see page 74), Dekay's Brownsnake (see page 55), and Common Wormsnake (see page 87).

How to tell apart from Smooth Earthsnakes (see page 128).

For more information on Flat-headed Snakes, see Ernst and Ernst (p. 346), Gibbons (p. 96), Phillips et al. (p. 248), Powell et al. (p. 398).

22. Common Watersnake

Scientific name	*Nerodia sipedon*
Size	Medium
Cottonmouth ratio	1,000+:1
Appearance of young	Young appear different from adults
Probability of seeing one	Negligible

Common Watersnakes, although fairly ubiquitous through-out southern Illinois, are almost never observed at Snake Road. When confronted by a potential predator, they tend to flee or hold their ground and perform what looks like a Northern Cottonmouth impression, flattening out the head and narrowing the neck. If you see one at Snake Road, count yourself among the lucky few. This snake is spotted even more rarely than Red-bellied Mudsnakes—I've never met anyone who's seen more than one Common Watersnake at Snake Road ever.

In a reversal of the usual order of things, these snakes become more colorful as they mature, not less. Juvenile coloration is typically dull, lacking the rich orange that can be seen on most adults. If you really want to observe a

Common Watersnake in southern Illinois, leave Snake Road and try walking the shores around small ponds or along the banks of rocky streams.

Common Water-snakes have orange bars on the margins of their lip scales.

Common Watersnakes have keeled scales.

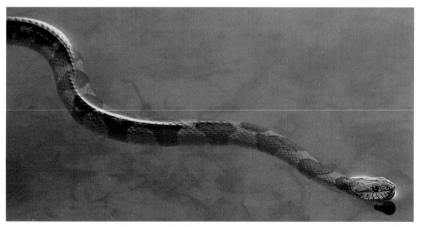

Common Watersnakes are highly aquatic and are most often found near or in ponds and streams.

Left, baby Common Watersnakes are heavily banded and show little or none of the orange coloration seen on adults. *Below*, young Common Watersnakes are very similar to young Plain-bellied Watersnakes, which are far more frequently observed at Snake Road. If you see a baby water-snake with strongly contrasting black and tan bands, you're almost certainly looking at a Plain-bellied Watersnake.

Although often brilliantly orange and yellow, Common Watersnakes can look rather dull when dirty, dry, or nearing the time to shed.

Similar to Eastern Copperhead (see page 65), Eastern Milksnake (see page 90), Northern Cottonmouth (see page 30), Diamond-backed Watersnake (see page 93), Mississippi Green Watersnake (see page 62), and Plain-bellied Water-snake (see page 36).

How to tell apart from Eastern Copperhead (see page 134).

For more information on Common Watersnakes, see Ernst and Ernst (p. 246), Gibbons (p. 250), Phillips et al. (p. 232), Powell et al. (p. 420).

23. Scarletsnake

Florida specimen; photograph courtesy of Jake Scott.

Scientific name	*Cemophora coccinea*
Size	Small
Cottonmouth ratio	Unknown
Appearance of young	Young resemble smaller adults
Probability of seeing one	Unknown

The Scarletsnake is Snake Road's greatest mystery and something of a controversy. A Scarletsnake has not been observed in the wild in Illinois since 1942, and even then, it was only a single specimen. All photographs in this section are Florida or Missouri specimens. Given that Scarletsnakes are more active at night, spend much of the time buried or beneath ground cover, and aren't known to migrate to survive the winter, it's conceivable that the species could go unnoticed for long periods of time. However, it is also possible that this species no longer inhabits the state of Illinois, or perhaps never did. Keep in mind that Scarletsnakes closely resemble Eastern Milksnakes (see page 90). The two species can be easily confused, even from a short distance. If you see a

Scarletsnakes have a wedge-shaped head that looks comparatively small for the body, and the lip scales have no bars or other dark markings. The top of the head down to the tip of the nose is red or orange. *Florida specimen; photograph courtesy of Jake Scott.*

Left, Scarletsnakes are covered in alternating blotches of black and red on a white or yellow background, and their scales are smooth. This animal has small lesions on its lip scales. Some snakes you encounter will bear scars, sores, or other evidence of a life spent in the wild. *Missouri specimen; photograph courtesy of Peter Paplanus. Right,* although usually vividly colored, Scarletsnakes grow dull as the time to shed the skin approaches. *Missouri specimen; photograph courtesy of Mike Pingleton.*

brightly colored red and black snake at Snake Road, it's more than likely an Eastern Milksnake, not a Scarletsnake.

Similar to Eastern Milksnake (see page 90), Eastern Copperhead (see page 65), and Common Watersnake (see page 105).

How to tell apart from an Eastern Milksnake (see page 138).

For more information on Scarletsnakes, see Ernst and Ernst (p. 60), Gibbons (p. 113), Phillips et al. (p. 196), Powell et al. (p. 367).

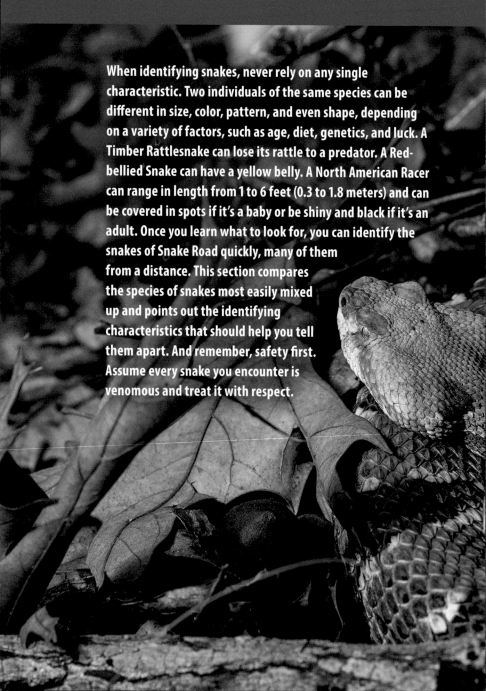

PART 2
HOW TO TELL SIMILAR SNAKES APART

When identifying snakes, never rely on any single characteristic. Two individuals of the same species can be different in size, color, pattern, and even shape, depending on a variety of factors, such as age, diet, genetics, and luck. A Timber Rattlesnake can lose its rattle to a predator. A Red-bellied Snake can have a yellow belly. A North American Racer can range in length from 1 to 6 feet (0.3 to 1.8 meters) and can be covered in spots if it's a baby or be shiny and black if it's an adult. Once you learn what to look for, you can identify the snakes of Snake Road quickly, many of them from a distance. This section compares the species of snakes most easily mixed up and points out the identifying characteristics that should help you tell them apart. And remember, safety first. Assume every snake you encounter is venomous and treat it with respect.

Black Snakes

Adding an extra layer of challenge to identifying the snakes of Snake Road, 8 of the 23 species can be described as "black snakes." Many of these snakes are not actually black, but that doesn't help much when you're observing them at a distance and in low light. In the dark, every snake is black. When you see a black snake at Snake Road, it will probably be one of these 8. They are listed in order of most likely encountered to least likely encountered.

Left, Northern Cottonmouth (venomous) (see page 30). A medium-sized, heavy-bodied snake with keeled scales and two-toned eyes. When threatened, Northern Cottonmouths gape, showing the white interior of the mouth. *Right*, Plain-bellied Watersnake (see page 36). A large, heavy-bodied snake with keeled scales and black bars on the margins of the lip scales.

Above left, Ring-necked Snake (see page 44). A very small, slender snake with smooth scales and a distinctive yellow or orange ring around the neck. *Above right*, Gray Ratsnake (see page 51). A large snake with lightly keeled scales and dark bars on the lip scales. Usually black, some Gray Ratsnakes are covered in gray blotches. *Right*, North American Racer (see page 58). A large snake with prominent eyes and smooth scales. Some individuals are iridescent blue where the sides and belly meet.

Eastern Black Kingsnake (see page 84). A medium-sized snake with smooth scales, covered with white or cream speckles that are smaller toward the animal's back and larger toward the belly.

Red-bellied Mudsnake (see page 96). A medium-sized iridescent snake with smooth scales and bright red or orange belly color that extends up along the sides in a wave-like pattern.

Eastern Hog-nosed Snake (black variant) (see page 98). A medium-sized snake with keeled scales and a unique upturned nose.

Northern Cottonmouth (Venomous) and Plain-bellied Watersnake

Inconveniently, the two most frequently observed species of snakes at Snake Road look quite a bit alike. Northern Cottonmouths and Plain-bellied Watersnakes are born sporting light and dark bands that fade as they mature, leaving the adults generally plain and dark, although there are exceptions. Not helping matters is the Plain-bellied Watersnakes' ability to perform what looks like a Northern Cottonmouth impression when they're alarmed. The back of the jaw spreads out and the neck narrows, making the head appear triangular. Plain-bellied Watersnakes won't gape their mouths like a Northern Cottonmouth, but they will sometimes snap if approached. The easiest way to tell the difference between the two (especially from a distance) is to look at the snake's chin. Northern Cottonmouths will often hold the head perpendicular to the ground, revealing the chin, which is covered with a distinctive checkered pattern. Plain-bellied Watersnakes have white, unmarked chins, and they don't usually hold the head at an angle that reveals the chin.

Northern Cottonmouth

Plain-bellied Watersnake

Northern Cottonmouth

Northern Cottonmouths have a broad dark stripe on the head that starts at the eye and runs back to the neck.

Northern Cottonmouths have a checkered chin, and that checkering extends down to the neck and belly.

The bands on baby Northern Cottonmouths are dark at the edges and lighter toward the middle. They often contain one or more small dark spots in the center. The tip of the tail is yellow or light green.

Plain-bellied Watersnake

Plain-bellied Watersnakes have dark bars at the margins of the lip scales, which are usually orange or yellow.

Plain-bellied Watersnakes have a white chin that transitions into vibrant yellow or orange where it meets the body.

The bands on baby Plain-bellied Watersnakes are solid black or dark gray from edge to edge, and the tip of the tail is dark.

Northern Cottonmouth

Northern Cottonmouths often bend the neck at an angle, pointing the nose almost straight into the air.

Northern Cottonmouths have elliptical pupils, but don't trust this characteristic. In low light, pupils dilate, becoming almost round. A more reliable characteristic is their two-toned eyes, which are light at the top and dark at the bottom.

Northern Cottonmouths are known for a triangular head and slender neck, but on its own that characteristic isn't reliable for a positive identification. Instead, look for the eyes. A Northern Cottonmouth's eyes are not visible from directly above the snake's head; it is only from the sides or below that will you see them.

Plain-bellied Watersnake

Plain-bellied Watersnakes generally keep the head parallel to the ground.

Plain-bellied Watersnakes have round pupils, but don't rely on using pupil shape to identify a snake. There are better identifying characteristics to look for that don't require you to get quite so close.

Plain-bellied Watersnakes can flex their jaws and neck into a silhouette that's similar to that of a Northern Cottonmouth. They can't change the shape of the scales on their heads, however, which leave the eyes clearly visible from above the snake or from the sides, but not from directly below.

Northern Cottonmouth (Venomous) and Eastern Copperhead (Venomous)

To some people, every snake is either an Eastern Copperhead or a suspected Eastern Copperhead. At Snake Road, you should treat every snake as a Northern Cottonmouth or a suspected Northern Cottonmouth. For every 50 Northern Cottonmouths you encounter, you *might* see one Eastern Copperhead. The two species are closely related, both in the genus *Agkistrodon,* so they share many characteristics.

Adult Northern Cottonmouths and Eastern Copperheads are easier to tell apart than their young. Adult Northern Cottonmouths are much darker than Eastern Copperheads and have little or no visible banding on the back, whereas Eastern Copperheads are distinctly banded. Once you've seen a few of each in the wild, an Eastern Copperhead will stand out from a Northern Cottonmouth like a gold necklace next to an iron chain. However, individual snakes vary substantially. If you want to be sure of the species, start by looking at the animal's chin and throat, which is easier than it might sound. Both species tend to hold the head perpendicular to the ground, especially when sensing a potential threat—you. Northern Cottonmouths have a checkered chin, Eastern Copperheads have a plain chin.

A warning: some of the characteristics that distinguish one species from the other are minuscule and difficult to observe unless you are close to the snake. Approach venomous snakes with care, never get within striking distance, and keep in mind that most of the snakes you'll encounter at Snake Road are venomous. A good rule of thumb is to remain farther away than the length of the snake's body at a minimum, and it's wise to be generous when estimating that length. A better rule of thumb is to remain farther away than your own body length, because it's quite difficult to estimate a snake's body length at a glance, especially if the snake is coiled. Better yet, bring a pair of binoculars or snap a photo with your mobile phone. You can identify the snake later using a bigger screen or show the photo to someone with more experience identifying snakes.

Northern Cottonmouth

Northern Cottonmouths have a broad, dark stripe on the head that starts at the eye and runs back to the neck.

Northern Cottonmouths have a checkered chin and throat.

If a snake is holding its mouth open and staring you down, it's almost certainly a Northern Cottonmouth.

Eastern Copperhead

Eastern Copperheads have a narrow, dark line that starts at the eye and looks like a tall sideways letter V.

Apart from the dark V-shaped line on the sides of the head, Eastern Copperheads have a plain chin and throat.

Eastern Copperheads might snap or strike if you get too close, but they will not gape like a Northern Cottonmouth.

Young Northern Cottonmouths and Eastern Copperheads are probably the most commonly misidentified snakes at Snake Road. The more of them you see, however, the easier it becomes to tell them apart at a glance. The characteristics listed above can be used to differentiate both adult and baby Northern Cottonmouths from Eastern Copperheads, but baby snakes from both species look enough alike it's good to have a few more ways to tell them apart. And although baby venomous snakes are less dangerous than adults because of their shorter striking range, shorter fangs, and smaller venom supply, they are still dangerous. Give them plenty of space.

Northern Cottonmouth

Baby Northern Cottonmouth.

Eastern Copperhead

Baby Eastern Copperhead.

The edges of a young Northern Cottonmouth's bands are jagged, as if the bands were assembled from a mosaic of light and dark scales.

Eastern Copperheads, both young and mature, have bands with smooth edges and look as if they were painted over the scales. The distinctive triangular shape of the bands, thick at the base and narrow at the top, is also a strong hint that you're looking at an Eastern Copperhead.

Northern Cottonmouth

A Northern Cottonmouth's eyes have split coloration. The top third is light brown or gold and the bottom two-thirds are dark brown.

Eastern Copperhead

An Eastern Copperhead's eyes are usually yellow or orange and lightly speckled.

North American Racer and Gray Ratsnake

North American Racers and Gray Ratsnakes are large, predominantly black snakes routinely observed at Snake Road. They are among the more difficult species to tell apart, especially from a distance. Despite a roughly similar appearance, these two species generally behave rather differently. North American Racers are extremely alert, energetic snakes. They rarely allow an observer to approach without retreating. Gray Ratsnakes seem more inclined to freeze, relying on protective coloration to avoid notice. If a long, black snake allows you to approach, chances are good it's a Gray Ratsnake, but keep in mind that snakes are guided by typical modes of behavior, not bound by them. Sometimes a North American Racer will freeze and let you approach. Sometimes a Gray Ratsnake will posture or flee. Both species are adept climbers and can be observed in trees or bushes. If you're close enough to see the snake's head, the fastest way to tell the difference between these two species is to look at the lower lip scales. Gray Ratsnakes have dark bars on the margins of the lower lip scales. North American Racers have white lower lip scales with no markings.

North American Racer

Gray Ratsnake

North American Racer

North American Racers have tapered heads that are only slightly wider than the neck.

North American Racers have smooth scales that are lighter at the edges.

A North American Racer's eyes stand out. They have gold irises and look disproportionately large for the head.

Gray Ratsnake

Gray Ratsnakes have heads with blunt snouts that grow broader toward the back of the jaw.

Gray Ratsnakes have oblong, lightly keeled scales.

A Gray Ratsnake's eyes appear proportionate in size to the head.

North American Racer

North American Racers are shiny black or sometimes bluish, and in direct sunlight some appear iridescent blue along the sides.

North American Racers have white bellies.

Upper lip scales on North American Racers are white on the bottom and black at the top. The lower lip scales are solid white.

Gray Ratsnake

Many Gray Ratsnakes at Snake Road are black, but some have light blotches on their backs.

Gray Ratsnakes have bellies that start out white at the neck but grow darker and become covered by gray or black checks farther back.

Gray Ratsnakes have dark bars at the margins of the top and bottom lip scales. Sometimes they're faint; sometimes they're distinct.

Red-bellied Snake and Dekay's Brownsnake

Another pair of closely related species, this time in the genus *Storeria*, Red-bellied Snakes and Dekay's Brownsnakes are both small snakes with keeled scales. Individual snakes of these two species exhibit a remarkable variety of colors and patterns, especially Red-bellied Snakes. Fortunately, a few characteristics that are unique to each species can help you tell the difference between them. The most obvious differences are on the head. Start by looking for a single white scale on the upper lip, behind and below the eye. If that white scale is present, you're looking at a Red-bellied Snake. If there is no white scale, look for one or two dark spots directly below the eye, which suggest a Dekay's Brownsnake.

Red-bellied
Snake

Dekay's
Brownsnake

Red-bellied Snake

Red-bellied Snakes have a single white scale on the upper lip, just behind and below the eye.

Red-bellied Snakes often have a light spot at the base of the head, sometimes flanked by two more small spots, one on each side of the neck.

The three spots at the base of the head can sometimes merge and look like a collar.

Dekay's Brownsnake

Below each eye, Dekay's Brownsnakes have one or two dark, triangular spots.

Dekay's Brownsnakes often have a pair of dark blotches at the base of the head.

On darker individuals, the blotches at the base of the head might be faint or invisible.

Western Ribbonsnake and Common Gartersnake

Western Ribbonsnakes and Common Gartersnakes are both dark, slender snakes with three distinct stripes running the length of the body. To help you learn the differences, their English names offer a useful mnemonic. Ribbons are delicate and decorative; Western Ribbonsnakes are slender and vividly colored. Garters are load bearing and functional; Common Gartersnakes have thicker bodies with muted colors. Both animals are among the most cold-tolerant snakes at Snake Road and can be spotted early in the spring and late in the fall—times when many other species are inactive. A quick way to tell these two similar species apart is to look at the upper lip scales. Common Gartersnakes have small bars or spots at the margins of some of the upper lip scales. Western Ribbonsnakes do not. Western Ribbonsnakes are among the most commonly observed snakes of Snake Road, while Common Gartersnakes are among the least commonly observed.

Western Ribbonsnake

Common Gartersnake

Western Ribbonsnake

Western Ribbonsnakes have lip scales that are solid cream or white, with no spots or bars.

The stripes on a Western Ribbonsnake's sides are light yellow or cream. The stripe down the middle of the back is often bright orange but sometimes also light yellow or cream.

Between the yellow stripes, Western Ribbonsnakes are usually solid black, although some individuals have little pale flecks scattered along the sides.

Common Gartersnake

Common Gartersnakes have two or three black bars or spots on the margins of the lip scales.

All three of a Common Gartersnake's stripes are usually the same color, typically white or pale yellow.

The black stripes on a Common Gartersnake's back are covered in sets of pale horizontal bars. These are sometimes interspersed with red flecks.

Smooth Earthsnake and Flat-headed Snake

Smooth Earthsnakes and Flat-headed Snakes are both small, inconspicuous, burrowing snakes with smooth scales. You can sometimes use color to tell the difference between these two species, unlike many other snakes that are similar to each other. Smooth Earthsnakes at Snake Road come in two main variants, gray and brown, while Flat-headed Snakes are always tan or golden brown. A small, smooth-scaled, light gray snake is a Smooth Earthsnake, not a Flat-headed Snake. But if the snake is smooth scaled and brown, you need to look at the head for a positive identification. Flat-headed Snakes really do have flat, wedge-shaped heads, which are usually a few shades darker than the body. Flat-headed

Smooth Earthsnake

Flat-headed Snake

Snakes are very rarely observed on Snake Road, so if you see a small, smooth-scaled, glossy brown snake, you're almost certainly looking at a Smooth Earthsnake. If you're still in doubt, look at the eyes. Flat-headed Snakes have small, black eyes with no visible iris. Smooth Earthsnakes have eyes that are comparatively large for their heads, and their irises are readily apparent.

Smooth Earthsnake

Flat-headed Snake

Smooth Earthsnakes have large eyes with visible irises.

Flat-headed Snakes have small, shiny black eyes without visible irises.

Smooth Earthsnakes have comparatively thick scales, giving them a textured appearance.

Flat-headed Snakes have scales that appear thin and almost interlocking, giving them a smooth appearance.

Common Wormsnake and Smooth Earthsnake

Apart from being small snakes, the Common Wormsnake and Smooth Earthsnake don't look especially alike when viewed side by side. At Snake Road, however, you're only likely to encounter them singly, and often in low light, which makes color much harder to discern. That can make it difficult to figure out which species you're looking at, especially since individuals of both species can sometimes be brown. The fastest and easiest way to tell the difference between the two is to look at the snake's side. Common Wormsnakes have bellies that are typically salmon or peach, which extends about a third of the way up the snake's side. Smooth Earthsnakes have pale and earth-toned bellies that aren't clearly visible from the side.

Common Wormsnake

Smooth Earthsnake

Common Wormsnake

Common Wormsnakes have eyes that are small and shiny black, without visible irises.

A Common Wormsnake's belly is typically salmon or peach, and this color extends perhaps a third of the way up the animal's side.

Smooth Earthsnake

Smooth Earthsnakes have large, almost bulbous eyes with visible irises.

From the side, you can see just the top of this Smooth Earthsnake's belly scales, which are slightly lighter than the snake's back.

Mississippi Green Watersnake and Diamond-backed Watersnake

Unless you can get close enough to see the scales around the eyes, these two species can be exceptionally difficult to tell apart. These snakes are both usually a shade of olive green (sometimes more green, sometimes more brown) with light and dark alternating bands along the sides. Although Diamond-backed Watersnakes have heavier bodies and grow much larger than Mississippi Green Watersnakes, this difference is only obvious in mature animals. Younger Diamond-backed Watersnakes are almost indistinguishable from Mississippi Green Watersnakes of all ages, especially

Mississippi Green Watersnake

This animal would be hard to tell from a young Diamond-backed Watersnake from a distance.

Diamond-backed Watersnake

Fully grown adults can reach or exceed 5 feet (1.5 meters) and grow noticeably thick around the middle.

from a distance. Mississippi Green Watersnakes are more frequently observed than Diamond-backed Watersnakes, however, so chances are good that if you see an olive-green watersnake with light and dark bands, it's a Mississippi Green Watersnake. If you can get close enough to make out minuscule details on the head, or if you brought a pair of binoculars, you can definitively identify the snake by looking for a tiny scale between the eye and the lip. Mississippi Green Watersnakes have this scale; Diamond-backed Watersnakes do not.

Mississippi Green Watersnake

Diamond-backed Watersnake

This Mississippi Green Watersnake is a typical specimen. The bands along the sides are only faintly visible.

Diamond-backed Watersnakes often have more pronounced bands than Mississippi Green Watersnakes, but not always. This Diamond-backed Watersnake's bands are only faintly visible.

The tiny rectangular scale directly under the eye and above the much larger lip scales definitively indicates the animal is a Mississippi Green Watersnake.

There is no scale directly between the eye and the lip scales of this Diamond-backed Watersnake. The lip scales are also separated by a dark bar at each margin.

Mississippi Green Watersnake and Diamond-backed Watersnake

Eastern Copperhead (Venomous) and Common Watersnake

Common Watersnakes are almost never observed on Snake Road, so if you're in doubt about whether you're looking at an Eastern Copperhead or a Common Watersnake, chances are good it's an Eastern Copperhead. At a glance, these two snakes share some broad commonalities. Both are medium sized, covered in bands, and earth-toned, and both have heavy bodies. Further, when alarmed, Common Watersnakes can widen the jaw and narrow the neck, lending the head a triangular silhouette reminiscent of a venomous snake. When threatened, the behaviors of both species are also similar. Both Eastern Copperheads and Common Watersnakes will sometimes coil and strike if approached. These strikes are often feints, but both snakes will bite if you get too close.

These two species differ in color, although it's subtle. Common Watersnakes tend to be orange and yellow, while Eastern Copperheads tends to be tan and pink, with only the back of the head taking on an orangey hue. Never rely on color to tell these two snakes apart, though. Some Eastern Copperheads look almost orange, while some Common Watersnakes can appear brown and tan, especially when they're getting ready to shed. Common Watersnakes and Eastern

Eastern Copperhead

Common Watersnake

Copperheads are both covered with dark bands over a lighter background, but you can quickly get an idea of which species you're looking at by checking the shape of the bands. On Eastern Copperheads, the bands are wide at the base and narrow at the top. On Common Watersnakes, the bands are narrow at the base and wide at the top.

Eastern Copperhead

Common Watersnake

Eastern Copperheads have a narrow but distinct sideways V on the side of the head and fine speckles on the lip scales.

Common Watersnakes have orange bars on the margins of the lip scales.

Adult Eastern Copperheads tend to have thick, heavy bodies, especially when compared to the head and neck.

Adult Common Watersnakes have thick, heavy bodies, much like adult Eastern Copperheads. This individual recently consumed a large meal, making it appear even chubbier than usual.

Eastern Copperhead

Because of the shape of the scales on the top of the head, Eastern Copperheads have eyes that are visible only from below the snake or from the side, not from directly above.

Eastern Copperheads have bands that are narrow toward the top of the back and thicker toward the belly. On some Eastern Copperheads, the bands don't cross the top of the back, leaving a gap.

Common Watersnake

Like all watersnakes at Snake Road, Common Watersnakes have eyes that are visible from directly above the snake or from the sides, but not from directly below.

Common Watersnakes have bands that are thick and unbroken across the back and narrower on the sides.

Eastern Copperhead

Baby Eastern Copperheads look like smaller adults. The bands on baby and adult Eastern Copperheads grow darker at their margins and lighter in the center. Sometimes, but not always, there is a small, dark spot in the middle of each band.

Common Watersnake

Baby Common Watersnakes look very different from adults. Their bands are solid black or gray from edge to edge.

The tip of the tail on baby Eastern Copperheads is yellow or green. This coloration fades to tan or brown as they mature.

The tails of baby Common Watersnakes are banded and exhibit the same color as the rest of the body.

Eastern Milksnake and Scarletsnake

Of the 23 species of snakes depicted in this book, Eastern Milksnakes and Scarletsnakes are possibly the most difficult to tell apart. However, a Scarletsnake has not been observed in the LaRue–Pine Hills region since 1942, and that one observation is problematic. Only one specimen was ever collected, and it was mislabeled for ten years before the error was discovered. The mislabeling of the specimen raises the possibility that other aspects of the record are incorrect. See Bennet (1953) for more information. Even if the record is accurate, it's spectacularly unlikely you'll encounter one. Nonetheless, it's worthwhile to learn the differences just in

Eastern
Milksnake

Scarletsnake

Florida specimen; photograph courtesy of Jake Scott.

case you get to be the one to rediscover this semi-mythical snake in Illinois.

Eastern Milksnakes and Scarletsnakes are strikingly similar in appearance, but there are a few notable differences. To start with, mature Eastern Milksnakes tend to have orange blotches, rather than red, and at their full adult size of over 3 feet (1 meter) in length, they are simply too large to be a Scarletsnake, which seldom exceeds 2 feet (0.6 meters) in length. To make a positive identification, however, you'll need to get close enough to make out small details, especially the shape of the head. Scarletsnakes have a pointed snout,

Eastern Milksnake

Scarletsnake

Eastern Milksnakes have a blunt snout and dark bars on the margins of the lip scales. The color of an Eastern Milksnake's snout might be solid red or orange, but it can also be white or yellow, disrupted by small patches of color.

Scarletsnakes have a pointed snout, which is solid red or orange all the way from between the eyes to the tip of the nose. A white or yellow snout suggests the animal is probably not a Scarletsnake. *Florida specimen; photograph courtesy of Jake Scott.*

This Eastern Milksnake's snout is almost entirely red. While a tricolored snake with a white or yellow snout is almost certainly an Eastern Milksnake, a tricolored snake with an entirely red snout could be either an Eastern Milksnake or a Scarletsnake. If the snout is red, check the head shape and the color on the lip scales.

and the margins of the lip scales are pale and unmarked. In contrast, Eastern Milksnakes have a blunt snout, and the margins of the lip scales typically have dark bars. The basic pattern of colors on the body is the same in both species: relatively wide red or orange blotches edged with black, separated by white or yellow. With Eastern Milksnakes, the black edging traces the red blotches all the way around, sometimes growing narrow toward the snake's belly. With Scarletsnakes, the black edging is most distinct on the top of the snake's back, becoming narrow or vanishing completely as it nears the snake's belly. It's always important to look for multiple characteristics when identifying a snake, but that should go double for distinguishing an Eastern Milksnake from a Scarletsnake.

Eastern Milksnake

The red or orange blotches on an Eastern Milksnake's back and sides extend below the animal's midline, sometimes reaching down to the edge of the belly. They are usually ringed by black, narrowing somewhat toward the bottom of each blotch. Be careful: the differences in how the red blotches are ringed by black can vary among individuals. Do not rely on the shape or position of the blotches to make an identification.

Scarletsnake

The red blotches on a Scarletsnake end at or just below the animal's midline. They are ringed almost all the way around by black, which is thickest toward the top of the snake's back and becomes thin or absent as it nears the belly. *Missouri specimen; photograph courtesy of Peter Paplanus.*

As Eastern Milksnakes mature, the red blotches fade to orange. At Snake Road, a snake that's over 3 feet (1 meter) long with bright orange blotches is always an Eastern Milksnake.

SOME FINAL THOUGHTS
SPECIES CHECKLIST
FURTHER READING

Some Final Thoughts

I have a lot of hopes for this book. I hope it will dispel some harmful myths about snakes. I hope it will help aspiring snake watchers have more productive and fulfilling visits to Snake Road. And I especially hope it will inspire others to do their part to protect the snakes and other wildlife of Snake Road. To me, and to many others, Snake Road is an almost spiritual place, where we go to get away from the cares of the world and appreciate the beauty of nature, especially snakes. Many of us have found not just snakes there, but also a warm and welcoming community of fellow snake enthusiasts. Snake Road has made my life immeasurably richer, and I can only end this book by paraphrasing Norman Maclean, a fellow lover of the outdoors: Like many snake watchers in southern Illinois where the spring sunlight only reaches below the bluff around midday, I often do not start snake watching until early afternoon. Then in the leaf-filtered twilight at the foot of Pine Hills Bluff, all existence fades to a being of my soul and memories and the songs of frogs and the hope of seeing a snake.

Eventually, all things merge into one, and Snake Road runs through it. The cottonmouths seek crevices that were cut into limestone, accumulated in the world's great flood, and hide from winter beneath rocks from the basement of time. Under some of the rocks are the wormsnakes, and sometimes a copperhead.

I am haunted by mudsnakes.

Species Checklist

No.	Common Name and Scientific Name	Page No.	Date and Time	Notes
1	Northern Cottonmouth (*Agkistrodon piscivorus*)	30		
2	Plain-bellied Watersnake (*Nerodia erythrogaster*)	36		
3	Western Ribbonsnake (*Thamnophis proximus*)	40		
4	Ring-necked Snake (*Diadophis punctatus*)	44		
5	Rough Greensnake (*Opheodrys aestivus*)	48		
6	Gray Ratsnake (*Pantherophis spiloides*)	51		
7	Dekay's Brownsnake (*Storeria dekayi*)	55		

No.	Common Name and Scientific Name	Page No.	Date and Time	Notes
8	North American Racer (*Coluber constrictor*)	58		
9	Mississippi Green Watersnake (*Nerodia cyclopion*)	62		
10	Eastern Copperhead (*Agkistrodon contortrix*)	65		
11	Timber Rattlesnake (*Crotalus horridus*)	69		
12	Red-bellied Snake (*Storeria occipitomaculata*)	74		
13	Smooth Earthsnake (*Virginia valeriae*)	78		
14	Common Gartersnake (*Thamnophis sirtalis*)	81		
15	Eastern Black Kingsnake (*Lampropeltis nigra*)	84		

No.	Common Name and Scientific Name	Page No.	Date and Time	Notes
16	Common Wormsnake (*Carphophis amoenus*)	87		
17	Eastern Milksnake (*Lampropeltis triangulum*)	90		
18	Diamond-backed Watersnake (*Nerodia rhombifer*)	93		
19	Red-bellied Mudsnake (*Farancia abacura*)	96		
20	Eastern Hog-nosed Snake (*Heterodon platirhinos*)	98		
21	Flat-headed Snake (*Tantilla gracilis*)	102		
22	Common Watersnake (*Nerodia sipedon*)	105		
23	Scarletsnake (*Cemophora coccinea*)	108		

Further Reading

Ballard, S. (1994). *Status of the herpetofauna in the La Rue–Pine Hills/Otter Pond Research Natural Area in Union County, Illinois* [Unpublished master's thesis]. Southern Illinois University Carbondale.

Bennett, E. (1953). An Illinois record of the scarlet snake. *Herpetologica 9*(4): 164.

Crother, B. I. (Ed.). (2017). *Scientific and standard English names of amphibians and reptiles of North America north of Mexico, with comments regarding confidence in our understanding* (8th ed.). Herpetological Circular no. 43. Society for the Study of Amphibians and Reptiles.

Ernst, C., & Ernst, E. (2003). *Snakes of the United States and Canada*. Smithsonian Books.

Gibbons, W. (2017). *Snakes of the eastern United States*. University of Georgia Press.

Gordon, W. (1963). *The cottonmouth (*Ancistrodon piscivorus leucostoma-Troost*) at Pine Hills, Union County, Illinois* [Unpublished master's thesis]. Southern Illinois University Carbondale.

Newcomb, Joe. (1973). [Interview with D. Michel about Larue–Pine Hills wilderness area management.] *Insight* [Radio program]. Anna, IL: WRAJ. Retrieved from Southern Illinois University Special Collections Research Center.

Palis, J. (2016). Snakes of "Snake Road." *Bulletin of the Chicago Herpetological Society 51*(1): 1–9. http://www.chicago herp.org/bulletin/51(1).pdf

Palis, J. (2018). An update on the snakes of Snake Road: Additionally-detected species and a comparison of spring and autumn observations. *Bulletin of the Chicago Herpetological Society 53*(5): 111–114. http://www.chicagoherp org/bulletin/53(5).pdf

Phillips, C., Brandon, R., & Moll, E. (1999). *Field guide to amphibians and reptiles of Illinois* (manual 8). Illinois Natural History Survey.

Powell, R., Conant, R., & Collins, J. (2016). *Peterson field guide to reptiles and amphibians of eastern and central North America* (4th ed.). Houghton Mifflin Harcourt.

Rossman, D. (1960). Herpetofaunal survey of the Pine Hills area of southern Illinois. *Quarterly Journal of the Florida Academy of Sciences 22*(4): 207–225.

Smith, P. (1961). The amphibians and reptiles of Illinois. *Illinois Natural History Survey Bulletin, 28*(1): 1–298.

Snake migration LaRue-Pine Hills [PDF]. (2006). https://www.fs.usda.gov/Internet/FSE_DOCUMENTS/stelprdb5106391.pdf

Joshua J. Vossler is an associate professor and academic librarian at Southern Illinois University Carbondale. He is a coauthor of *Humor and Information Literacy: Practical Techniques for Library Instruction*, specializes in making instructional videos about research skills, and is a lifelong snake watcher.

 *A Shawnee Book*

Also available in this series . . .

*The Next New Madrid Earthquake:
A Survival Guide for the Midwest*
WILLIAM ATKINSON

*Reckoning at Eagle Creek: The Secret
Legacy of Coal in the Heartland*
JEFF BIGGERS

*History as They Lived It: A Social
History of Prairie du Rocher, Illinois*
MARGARET KIMBALL BROWN

*Foothold on a Hillside: Memories
of a Southern Illinoisan*
CHARLESS CARAWAY

*Growing Up in a Land Called Egypt:
A Southern Illinois Family Biography*
CLEO CARAWAY

*Colonial Ste. Genevieve: An
Adventure on the Mississippi Frontier*
CARL J. EKBERG

*A Nickel's Worth of Skim Milk:
A Boy's View of the Great Depression*
ROBERT J. HASTINGS

*A Penny's Worth of Minced
Ham: Another Look at
the Great Depression*
ROBERT J. HASTINGS

Southern Illinois Coal: A Portfolio
C. WILLIAM HORRELL

*Always of Home: A Southern
Illinois Childhood*
EDGAR ALLEN IMHOFF

*Lives of Fort de Chartres:
Commandants, Soldiers, and
Civilians in French Illinois,
1720–1770*
DAVID MACDONALD

*Kaskaskia: The Lost
Capital of Illinois*
DAVID MACDONALD AND
RAINE WATERS

*20 Day Trips in and around the
Shawnee National Forest*
LARRY P. AND DONNA J. MAHAN

*Land of Big Rivers: French and
Indian Illinois, 1699–1778*
M. J. MORGAN

*America's Deadliest Twister:
The Tri-State Tornado of 1925*
GEOFF PARTLOW

*Escape Betwixt Two Suns:
A True Tale of the Underground
Railroad in Illinois*
CAROL PIRTLE

Fishing Southern Illinois
ART REID

*All Anybody Ever Wanted of
Me Was to Work: The Memoirs
of Edith Bradley Rendleman*
EDITH BRADLEY RENDLEMAN
EDITED BY JANE ADAMS

*The Civilian Conservation Corps
in Southern Illinois, 1933–1942*
KAY RIPPELMEYER

*Giant City State Park and the
Civilian Conservation Corps:
A History in Words and Pictures*
KAY RIPPELMEYER

*Fluorspar Mining: Photos from
Illinois and Kentucky, 1905–1995*
HERBERT K. RUSSELL

*A Southern Illinois Album:
Farm Security Administration
Photographs, 1936–1943*
HERBERT K. RUSSELL

*The State of Southern Illinois:
An Illustrated History*
HERBERT K. RUSSELL